WITHDRAWN

STORIED CITIES of JAPAN

TOKYO

YOKOHAMA

KAMAKURA

KYOTO

NARA

OSAKA

KOBE

NAGASAKI

❀ KAZUO NISHIDA ❀

STORIED CITIES
of JAPAN

JOHN WEATHERHILL, INC.
Tokyo

Published by John Weatherhill, Inc., 50 Ryudo-cho, Azabu, Minato-ku, Tokyo, Japan. / Copyright in Japan, 1963, by John Weatherhill, Inc. All rights reserved. / Printed in Japan. / First edition, November, 1963.

Table of Contents

5

TABLE OF CONTENTS

List of Photographs

Foreword

SEVERAL YEARS AGO, AS I WAS STANDING before a small pavilion near the Hachiman Shrine in Kamakura, a group of Western tourists arrived for sightseeing in that ancient center of civilization. After a glance at the structure, they continued on to inspect other sights. From the remarks which I overheard, I gathered that they wondered what this "quaint-looking relic" was, and if it had any story to tell out of Kamakura's rich past.

The structure, of course, was the Maidono, the Pavilion of the Dance, where eight centuries ago a lovely and tragic woman performed the most famous dance in Japanese history. The woman, Lady Shizuka, was a *shirobyoshi,* the ancient term for dancer, and today she is regarded as the spiritual ancestor of the modern geisha. She was also the lover of the great and youthful general Yoshitsune, who was then at war with his half brother Yoritomo, the dictator of Kamakura. And the dance which Lady Shizuka performed on this same platform so many years ago took place after she had been taken captive by her lover's mortal enemy; it was a dance commanded by and defiant of Yoritomo, a dance praising the virtues of Yoshitsune and pledging eternal loyalty to him.

Although familiar to every Japanese school child, the story of Lady Shizuka is practically unknown to the ordinary visitor to Japan. The usual guide book has no room for information of this kind; flat statistics and itineraries demand that space. Thus for the majority of foreign visitors, the Maidono remains inert, and is remembered, if at all, as "that quaint-looking relic."

The realization that there is a void here which should be filled, and that the stories behind Japan's landmarks and monuments can prove both profitable and interesting to English-speaking persons who are not specialists in Japanese history—this was the genesis of this modest work. I have selected and related these tales of Japan, not only for globe-trotters who may come here, but also for the many others who stay at home but remain eager to learn something of this storied land of the East.

History and legend have become closely wedded in the passing of many centuries in Japan, and often it is difficult to separate them. Where ambiguity exists, I have endeavored to ascertain and convey the historical facts rather than creations of the imagination, however intriguing these latter may be. But I have by no means attempted to eliminate the legends entirely, for these too serve a cultural purpose and add richly to the country's reservoir of treasures. Japan is particularly fortunate in this respect, for it is an old country whose poets, writers, and playwrights have, by their genius, made legends immortal. I have regarded it as my task, therefore, not to make these two categories mutually exclusive, but simply to indicate their approximate domains.

And so this book is mainly historical, with a number of legends added. It is also contemporary in so far as the matters which have been selected for discussion will give an added dimension, that of time, to the things which the visitor may see, the places he may visit, in present-day Japan. In each of the chapters I have also made it a point to describe, not only the events of the past which give each place its history and personality, but also the contemporary atmosphere of that place which a visitor might expect to find should he go there today. If this book contributes, however slightly, to man's thirst for knowledge and understanding, particularly in respect to Japan's colorful past and changing present, I shall consider my efforts repaid.

I wish to acknowledge here the many people who were involved in the preparation of this manuscript, and to express my gratitude to them. The various chapters of this book first appeared in serial form in the magazine *Asia Scene,* published by Nihon Kogyo Shimbun (Japan Industrial Journal); for their cooperation in this present compilation, I thank the officers of that organization, and in particular Eikichi Araki, board chairman, and Hidezo Inaba, president. I also wish to acknowledge the helpful assistance of Tamotsu Yamamoto and Shozo Hochi, managing editor and editor respectively of *Asia Scene*, and the *Japan Times*, which kindly gave me access to its files. The majority of the photographs used in the text were obtained from the Japan Travel Bureau, and I am grateful to Katsuji Yabuki of that organization for his advice and suggestions. The photos which appear on pages 110-11 were taken by Naoya Inouye. To Ian Dunlop and John Dower I express my gratitude for their valuable contributions in editing, and to Yasuko Dower for her fine suggestions concerning translation of the poems which appear in Chapter 13.

KAZUO NISHIDA

PART 1

TOKYO

1

The Castle

and Its Residents

SEEN AT NIGHT FROM THE TOP OF TOKYO Tower, the Japanese capital glitters below like a limitless sea of light. Crisscrossed by ribbons of neon lighting, the city that is forever awake and forever on the move seems to cover the entire Kanto Plain.

Like a lady of uncertain age, Tokyo is fairest after dark. Then the city is alive, sparkling, gay. Along its avenues, auto headlights stop and start, turning and twisting, weaving a magic spiderweb in the dark. High above them the light-studded buildings stand in serried ranks all around the Imperial Palace.

So careless and carefree is the city's demeanor, so vivid its air of prosperity, that a visitor to these shores can now hardly believe this was the place that was laid in charred ruins in the dreadful holocaust that wiped out large areas of the city in the last stages of the Pacific War. Those were grim days, and the perils of the time are still etched deeply in the memories of its citizens.

Before peace came at last in August, 1945, nearly a million homes had been destroyed and 160,000 more demolished to provide firebreaks and avenues of escape during air raids. The population, meanwhile, had dwindled down to a mere 2,400,000, from a total of more than five million persons who had been residents of Tokyo at the outbreak of the war.

The city's rebirth from the ashes of war was as spectacular as its wartime disasters. Tokyo has not only been completely rebuilt, but in the current surge of the nation's economy, buildings are rising up ever bigger and more handsome. With a population approaching the ten million mark, Tokyo is not only the first city of the Far East but is now the world's largest metropolis.

Administratively, Tokyo is a maze of districts and inter-locking entities. It embraces twenty-three wards, ten cities, three counties, and three territorial offices whose furthermost islands in the Izu Archipelago lie more than 185 miles away, far to the south in the Pacific Ocean. To most of its inhabitants, Tokyo is a city of traffic jams and crowded quarters, yet the mountains beyond the Ogochi Dam still harbor wild game, including deer, monkeys, and wild boar —all within the limits of the metropolis.

Tokyo has rivers, mountains, plains, islands. It has three main rivers, the Tama-gawa, Sumida-gawa, and Edo-gawa, all fed by the snows of the Chichibu Mountains. In the upper reaches of these rivers eels swim, carp play, and *ayu* trout flash their silvery scales in pellucid waters, a lure for anglers from the busy city.

After splashing through the gorges of their upper regions, these historic streams cross the populous plain in leisurely fashion and finally empty into Tokyo Bay. Together with their tributaries, they annually carry vast alluvial deposits to the city's doorstep, so that Tokyo may be said to be crawling continually southward, like a living creature, providing new lands in the shallow bay for mushrooming factories. As proof of this timeless terrestrial flow, the southern approaches to Ginza and Tsukiji, now occupied by shops and concrete buildings, were once under water. Even as late as the era of Tokugawa Ieyasu in the sixteenth century, an inlet of the bay came right up to where the Imperial Palace now stands, and what is today Hibiya Park was then a marsh where wildfowl in great numbers greeted fishermen returning from the sea.

Tokyo is not only the home of the emperor and the seat of government, it is also the nation's financial, educational, and publishing capital. It is the center of the country's art, theater, and sports. From the Japanese Wall Street at Nihombashi, the great men of industry direct their empires. The city richly rewards its gifted men, but it deals harshly with mediocrity. All the nation's talented—and not-so-talented—people are drawn here irresistibly in the search for fame and fortune.

Tokyo is the head, the brains, the lifeblood of the nation. So enormous is the concentration of activity that the rest of the country would lie helpless, like a decapitated serpent, were Tokyo ever to be severed or destroyed. The hinterlands would still survive perhaps, but they would never regain their full stature without Tokyo. Here gather the nation's leaders, the alert and the enterprising, building both visible and invisible structures of bewildering complexity. They wield their power, whether for good or evil, with skill and boldness, in such crucial domains as finance and politics. These men and the edifices they build attract more people, more vehicles, more factories, and more of everything in this world's most congested beehive. The result is that Tokyo today is more indispensable to the country that nourishes it than either New York or London to theirs.

Viewed from above, the city's rail arteries are laid in the form of a giant salamander. There is first the Loop Line

17

around which Yamate trains speed endlessly, forming the fat, round body of the amphibian. Right through its center, beginning at Tokyo Station in the heart of the city, stretches the Central Line that constitutes the monster's spine and tail. This line rolls westward through Shinjuku and out to Tachikawa, Hachioji, and points beyond.

As if this creature were being snagged by a giant hand, the Tokaido Line comes from the south right up to the monster's mouth at Tokyo Station, the focal point of all rail traffic in eastern Japan. In addition to the main lines, a complex network of other lines flows outward from the city's heart like the rays in a child's drawing of the sun.

Because of the extreme density of population in this area, the congestion at railway stations is a continual problem. More than a million people swarm into the middle of the city each day from the suburbs and the four surrounding prefectures, crowding the platforms, jamming the coaches, and making each rush-hour ride an ordeal. The long-suffering commuters are resigned to this daily ordeal as part of the burden of modern life. They rush through the train doors that open and close automatically, sometimes squeezing a stray body or two; they hang desperately to overhead straps in crowded coaches that roar away with hair-splitting regularity, each train spaced scarcely two minutes apart at rush hours.

On the roads, too, the fast tempo of Tokyo's growth has created enormous problems for the civic planners. The plain fact is that there are more vehicles in the streets than there is room for. The result is that on any busy day the traffic stalls interminably at intersections, fraying tempers all around.

To ease this situation, some bold plans have been put forward, some of them on a tremendous scale which, if carried out, would radically affect both the character and appearance of the city. The more spectacular proposals are:

1. Removal of the political capital to some remote spot such as the foothills of Mt. Fuji or the plain of Nasu. This would siphon off a substantial part of Tokyo's population to the new center of administration and thus ease the population pressure.

2. Removal of the emperor's residence away from Tokyo, releasing its immense grounds for parks and through ways, thus not only relieving traffic in downtown districts, but also speeding up crosstown traffic which now must make a circuitous detour around the palace moats.

3. Leveling the mountains of nearby Chiba and using the earth to fill in Tokyo Bay, thus doubling the capital's land area for building model apartments, civic buildings, factories, etc.

4. Building up satellite cities around the perimeter of Tokyo.

All of these projects present enormous practical difficulties. Transferring the political capital elsewhere, for instance, would not only entail staggering costs, but would face strong opposition from vested interests whose livelihood depends upon preserving the *status quo*. With South America's Brasilia set before Tokyo's planners as a shining model, this project is immensely persuasive, but its full realization seems remote. Sections of the government offices, however, may be moved to the foothills of Mt. Fuji under a plan now under consideration.

There is general agreement that the second plan would speed up traffic. Militating against the scheme would be the strong sentimental reluctance to move the emperor, symbol of the people's unity, from his historic residence at the heart of the nation. Moreover, a new palace replacing the old structure that was destroyed in World War II is already under construction on the old site.

As a compromise solution, a plan to dig underground speedways beneath the palace grounds is being considered, but even this may not mature due chiefly to the high cost and the Japanese reluctance to encroach, however indirectly, upon the imperial preserve.

Scheme No. 3, to level the mountains and fill in Tokyo Bay, if realized, would constitute one of the greatest engineering feats of all time. It would be comparable in scale to the dream of Soviet engineers to block the narrows between Sakhalin and Siberia to produce warm weather for the whole of Eastern Siberia and Manchuria.

This Greater Tokyo Bay project, while it has many high-level advocates, seems also fated to remain indefinitely in the blueprint stage. It may be pointed out, however, that Tokyo Bay is actually being filled in all the time, although on a limited scale, both by the work of dredging engineers and the natural process of alluvial sedimentation mentioned earlier.

This leaves the satellite cities of Plan No. 4 as the only feasible alternative. Though modified for budgetary reasons, this project is nevertheless being pushed forward by the governor of Tokyo, Dr. Ryotaro Azuma, and his planners, particularly in connection with the surface speedways now under construction which are designed to join various satellite centers with the mother city before foreign visitors start converging on Tokyo for the 1964 Olympic Games.

The dominant feature of Tokyo, of course, is the Imperial Palace and the great moats surrounding it. The original Edo Castle situated here was built by a local chieftain named Ota Dokan in the fifteenth century. A bronze statue of him in the pose of an archer now stands in front of the City Hall. Dokan was at first an untutored rustic who showed more interest in subjugating the clansmen of Kanto than in the graces of court life. He was out hunting one day in the area where Takatanobaba Station now stands in Shinjuku ward, so the story goes, when his party was caught in a downpour of rain. While waiting for the shower to pass, he noted a peasant girl emerging from a hut. He asked her for a *mino* (straw raincoat). To his surprise the girl, with great politeness, presented him instead with a sprig of yellow roses, and then withdrew without a word.

Back in his castle, the puzzled baron asked his fellow huntsmen the meaning of the girl's action. He was told that an old poem described the glory of the wild rose that bloomed in profusion but which could produce not a single seed or, in Japanese, *mino hitotsu,* which sounds the same in the original tongue as " one straw raincoat."

It is said that Dokan was so perturbed by his ignorance of the girl's language of poetry that he thenceforth devoted much time to literature, becoming in time a famous scholar as well as a great warrior. This founder of Edo (now Tokyo) built the castle in 1456. He died at an assassin's hand thirty years later.

Despite Dokan's earlier contributions, the real founder of Edo, the man who built it into a great city, was the shogun Tokugawa Ieyasu, founder of the Tokugawa dynasty. Ieyasu was born in 1542, when his father, a petty baron, was only seventeen years old. Ill luck seemed to dog the future shogun (nation's military dictator) almost from the start. Ieyasu's father died when the boy was only seven, and his widowed mother remarried shortly afterwards, leaving the little son behind at his father's estate in Okazaki (now Aichi prefecture). Ieyasu was thus actually bereft of both parents at the age of eight, and for the moment his future seemed none too certain in those times of violently changing fortune.

Luckily for him, he was a sturdy lad with a toughness of spirit that carried him through the harsh early years. As he reached maturity, he grew in worldly wisdom. As a young man he joined forces with Oda Nobunaga, who was then a rising star among the feuding war lords in the neighborhood of Ieyasu's domains.

In this alliance of convenience, Ieyasu protected the rear while his fiercely ambitious partner pushed his columns eastward to the capital at Kyoto. There, Nobunaga, the big, brash autocrat of Owari Castle, crushed all opposition, becoming in fact the realm's first lord and dictator.

After Nobunaga's rise to power, Ieyasu and Toyotomi Hideyoshi, another ambitious man, became lieutenants of roughly equal rank in the service of their common lord. Although a resourceful leader with considerable skill as a general, Nobunaga had a vulnerable streak in his character. He was given to whims, often indulging in the risky game of ridicule. His partisan treatment of subordinates, particularly his jeering remarks to those who displeased him, stirred secret resentments among some of his followers. He aroused a gnawing hatred in Akechi Mitsuhide, who was ostensibly a devoted liegeman. Mitsuhide was an avaricious opportunist. He is sometimes described as the Benedict Arnold of Japan. Rising in wrath, in 1582 he destroyed Nobunaga's power at Honno-ji, a temple in Kyoto, in one of the country's most celebrated acts of perfidy, and there his erstwhile master died fighting in the temple as it went up in flames and his body was burned to ashes.

At the time of the *coup d'etat* Hideyoshi and Ieyasu were rivals for succession to Nobunaga's mantle. The more aggressive Hideyoshi quickly emerged supreme, however, by making a series of lightning attacks that broke Mitsuhide's power. With a judicious use of both force and political persuasion, Hideyoshi then rose to become Kampaku, the title signifying paramount authority which was bestowed upon him by the emperor.

All this while, Ieyasu cannily waited for his opportunity. It was long in coming, but he was a man who could wait. There is an old saying which is sometimes erroneously attributed to Ieyasu. Although of uncertain origin, it aptly expresses Ieyasu's basic creed. It goes: "One should never hurry this thing called life, which is like a man with a heavy burden on his shoulders traversing a long road ahead.''

Hideyoshi and Ieyasu were both strong leaders, each in a different way. The two men contrasted sharply. Hideyoshi was a master strategist, a man of inspired dash who not only liked to take calculated risks, but often took them at seemingly reckless odds. Luck seemed almost always to be riding by his side, for he had an original mind and was extremely flexible in operation. He kept ceaselessly expanding his realm, like a man charmed by his own successes, until he eventually spread his power even to Korea.

Ieyasu, on the other hand, was basically a cautious man. He remained in his stronghold in Kanto (East Japan), conserving his strength for the morrow. He was a good administrator, governing his fief wisely. He was thrifty, provident, careful. He not only preached the simple life but also lived it. His favorite saying was: "Regard all extravagance as your enemy."

Both Hideyoshi and Ieyasu amassed immense wealth, which consisted largely of gold and silver bullion. While Hideyoshi spent his wealth lavishly, Ieyasu used his own sparingly, even parsimoniously. His patience was proverbial. He waited for Nobunaga and Hideyoshi, his two predecessors, to unite the country by vast expenditures of wealth in wars. Only then, after they were both dead, was he prepared to strike for leadership. By that time the country they had pacified was ready for his plucking. Nevertheless, Ieyasu had to fight hard against other rivals, and he fought them with great energy and success.

When occasion demanded it, Ieyasu was a man who could be both bold and ruthless, but he is best known to history as the master of calculated cunning. Nicknamed Old Badger, he was a clever manager of worldly affairs. In the two tremendous battles he fought for mastery of the land, he won them both largely by subversion. At Sekigahara his victory was clinched by the defection of important elements in the enemy's ranks. In the decisive battle of Osaka Castle victory came only after his fifth columnists and his foxy Trojan War tactics made that renowned castle militarily untenable (for the story of this battle of Osaka Castle, see Chapter 14).

Modern critics are apt to take an acid view of Ieyasu as a man, but history has no illusions about his standing as the first statesman of his time. The socio-political edifice he reared endured for more than two and a half centuries after his death. The particular brand of feudalism he laboriously perfected, with himself at the apex of a pyramiding system of loyalties, was his own formula for self-perpetuating power, and it lasted after him for fourteen generations of his dynasty.

After the battle of Sekigahara (1600) and his appointment as shogun (1603), he began in earnest to build up Edo, transforming this former marshy village into a great political capital. He enlarged Edo Castle, which Ota Dokan had earlier built. Even after his retirement as shogun, he kept a firm hand on the reins of government as a shadow-dictator behind his son Hidetada. Ieyasu died in 1616, probably of stomach cancer.

The fifteen shogun in the Tokugawa line, which began with Ieyasu, were men of varying talents and dispositions. Some were powerful personalities, others were mediocrities. The third shogun, Iemitsu, for instance, was temperamentally the antithesis of his frugal grandfather. He was called Iemitsu the Magnificent. A lavish spender, he not only spent the hoard which Ieyasu had so prudently amassed for his successors, but he levied vast additional taxes to erect at Nikko the glittering Toshogu Shrine, where he enshrined his grandfather.

Another resident of Edo Castle was the fifth shogun,

Tsunayoshi, a man of a different color. Though a spoiled playboy and dilettante of no great ability, he loomed conspicuous in history because fate had designated him shogun at a period when Edo reached its golden age of culture. This was the dazzling epoch of Genroku. It was a time when beauty was prized and life was zestful, and the newly risen merchant class flowered as it had never done before.

Against this fashionable background, Tsunayoshi flourished in a grand manner. He considered himself a model of his age. He dabbled in literature. He fancied himself a Confucian scholar. He was given to whims and moods, often with unfortunate consequences.

Offended by what he considered a desecration of his residence, he summarily ordered the execution of Asano Takumi no Kami when that impetuous daimyo attacked a tormentor, Kira Kozukenosuke, after a quarrel in Edo Castle. Hot with rage, Tsunayoshi punished the wrong person at the wrong time, thus blackening his own name for posterity. This historical incident is the basis for the great drama of revenge called *The Forty-seven Loyal Retainers of Ako,* more familiar to Kabuki lovers as *Chushingura* and to Western readers as *The Forty-seven Ronin.*

Tsunayoshi is also remembered as the author of the Edict for Loving All Living Things. By this law, aimed chiefly at protecting dogs, he caused such a large increase in Edo's canine population that the situation got out of hand. Dogs of all kinds and all sizes were pampered and petted in such royal fashion, with anyone caught molesting them being given quick punishment, that the exasperated populace finally had its revenge by giving him the nickname Dog Shogun, a name which survives to this day.

One of the ablest shogun was Yoshimune, the eighth in the line. He was a great lawgiver. The fourth shogun, Ietsuna, was a mere child of eleven when he acquired his title.

But the ruler who lasted the longest and made the biggest splash in the decadent years of the early nineteenth century was Ienari. A strong-willed shogun, he had decidedly strong views about public morality—even though his own life was no model of rectitude. He made great ado about censorship, locking up famous *ukiyo-e* artists for publishing what he considered indecent or subversive pictures. Utamaro, one of the greatest of his craft, was a victim of this prudishness: he was handcuffed and locked up in his home for fifty days to appease Ienari's sense of moral outrage.

For all his efforts in this field, Ienari was no ordinary bluenose. In truth, he was more like a Japanese version of " Solomon in all his glory." He held his high office as a virtual dictator for forty-five years. He kept a harem of 606 concubines and begat 55 children (28 boys and 27 girls), and he once had a bridge spanning the pond in his garden made of sugar, a commodity which was then so expensive as to be beyond the reach of ordinary citizens.

The ruler who showed his statesmanship in a negative manner by giving up his power for the good of his country was the last shogun, Yoshinobu. The revolution of 1868 is known as the Restoration because, at least in outward form, it "restored" political authority to the emperor. It might have had catastrophic consequences in the form of a bloody war had the fifteenth shogun decided to fight it out against the loyalist forces who had raised the banner of the emperor and were even then swarming into Edo.

Though a man of peace, Yoshinobu had forces of fanatically loyal men under him to fight if he had chosen to do so, but he wisely refrained. After more than 250 years of power, the Bakufu—or military government—over which he presided was badly undermined. It was beset by financial difficulties, and shaken by domestic violence. It was also confronted by the demands of foreign powers for trade and concessions.   Even before the first skirmishes between his men and the loyalist forces, Yoshinobu decided to abdicate. He was content to retire gracefully from the scene, transferring his authority to the emperor, whose progenitors had traditionally reigned but not ruled from their old palace in Kyoto.

Yoshinobu left Edo Castle in February, 1868, retiring to Kanei-ji, a temple in Edo's Ueno Park. The real hero of that occasion, however, was Rintaro Katsu, Yoshinobu's navy minister. Returned from a voyage to the United States in Japan's first modern warship, this man of spare physique but iron will was gifted with perception and statesmanlike foresight. He was determined to prevent further bloodshed at all costs. He feared that all Edo would go up in flames if fighting broke out in the city.

As the shogun's chief adviser, he boldly entered the enemy headquarters, scorning all personal danger, and there he met General Takamori Saigo, whose statue looks down today from a height in Ueno Park. Saigo was one of the commanding generals of the loyalist forces which had earlier entered Edo, and the two men reached an agreement for the peaceful transfer of power.

Although Yoshinobu had acted to prevent Edo from becoming a battlefield, the more fanatical of his followers refused to capitulate. They formed the Corps of Justice (Shogitai) and fought a last-ditch battle in the hills of Ueno. That story is better told as part of the rich lore of that famous park, appearing in Chapter 7.

The imperial court was moved from Kyoto to Edo (shortly to be renamed Tokyo, or Eastern Capital) to indicate its new status, and Emperor Meiji, an enlightened sovereign, was the first emperor to reign from Edo Castle, now the Imperial Palace. His reign was long and notable, a period in which the country emerged for the first time as a modern power. He was succeeded by Emperor Taisho. The present emperor, the son of Emperor Taisho, ascended the throne in 1926.

Great vicissitudes of fortune marked the rule of the fifteen Tokugawa shogun and likewise the reigns of the three emperors who have lived in the palace since the Restoration. There have been wars and great natural disasters. Earthquakes, typhoons, fires, and bombings in the late war have shaken the city to its foundation. After each of these calamities, however, its citizens have always managed to rebuild their city.

As a metropolis born of Ieyasu's dream, Tokyo is a comparative newcomer. This certainly is true when contrasted with the ancient origins of Rome or London or even of Nara and Kyoto, since these older cities have memories that go back more than a thousand years.

Though only a little more than three centuries old, Tokyo has always been noted for the spirit of its citizens, whose expansive ways and exuberant energy have made it today the First City of the Far East and the largest in the world.

2

Ginza

Sons of Edo
on the Silver Way

GINZA IS THE GREAT SILVER WAY THAT RUNS
through the heart of Tokyo. Old with memories of historic
events, it is a remarkable district and its main street a remarkable thoroughfare. True, the street is shorter than New
York's Broadway. It is narrower than San Francisco's
Market Street. Its buildings are less imposing than those of
London or Paris.

But for all its physical limitations, Ginza has an air
about it that many find irresistible and a charm that is not
easily forgotten. It has sophistication, but not too much,
and it has the common touch but without vulgarity. It is
full of wares to meet all tastes; it has uncounted places for
enjoying the good things of life. It is without doubt the
queen of the Orient's shopping centers. It is a kind of
glorified bazaar, a place where peoples of all nations come

to buy things, from trinkets to houses and treasures of art. Ginza will beguile your heart, charm your palate—and leave you with a thin pocketbook. It is truly the Show Window of Asia.

To appraise Ginza's unique character fully, it is well to understand something of the people who created it in the centuries since Ieyasu made Edo his capital. Ginza is the finest handiwork of an enterprising race called Edokko (sons of Edo), who developed it from a footpath through a marsh to one of the most famous main streets in the world.

Historically, the Edokko were a long time in achieving a recognizable identity. Strengthened by the rise of the new merchant class, however, they were already flourishing at the time of the Genroku era in the late seventeenth century. In the etymological evolution of the term, Edokko originally referred to the ordinary townfolk, the merchants and artisans, as distinguished from the ruling aristocracy that poured into Edo after the first Tokugawa shogun, Ieyasu, arrived here to found his dynasty.

The ruling class was headed by the shogun, and consisted of the feudal barons, called daimyo, and the samurai retainers who served them. The samurai in particular appeared most conspicuous as they swaggered about town wearing two swords symbolizing their privileged status and authority. Their lords, though less numerous, were powerful figures with domains of their own, some of them in distant parts of the country. They enjoyed a considerable degree of autonomy, possessing armies of their own as well as the machinery to preserve order. Over them ruled the shogun, in pomp and splendor from the stronghold of Edo Castle.

To assure perpetuation of his power, the shogun devised many ingenious schemes. One of them deserves special attention because it made many an ambitious daimyo think twice before striking out for power against the shogunate.

The daimyo were required to establish domiciles in Edo in addition to their establishments in the provinces, and to keep either themselves or their families at all times in Edo, where agents of the shogun could keep a close watch on their every move.

This practice, known as *sankin kotai,* was of course an unsubtle form of hostage, but it worked. It deterred the daimyo, some of them of great power and wealth, from ever risking insurrection during the long Tokugawa peace that lasted for more than two and a half centuries.

The daimyo were constantly traveling from home to Edo and back again. This was an expensive business, often ruinous to their exchequer, but they deemed it necessary to travel in elaborate and costly procession for reasons of prestige. The shogun, needless to say, craftily encouraged these elaborate corteges on the premise that daimyo so burdened financially were less likely to start trouble for the regime he headed. In Edo these lords attended to state functions. Back home they were needed for overseeing their fiefs. In their journeys to and fro they traveled handsomely in mile-long processions consisting of palanquins, porters, and soldiers in full battle armor.

All along the way the captains of the guards were in the custom of calling out imperiously "Down on your knees!" to passers-by, commanding the plebeian order to kneel, heads to the ground, lest they be cut down on the spot for presuming to look at the august travelers.

All through the Edo age such processions passed back and forth along the whole length of what is now Ginza, from Shimbashi to Nihombashi. From Nihombashi the line of march swerved sharply westward toward the castle and the baronial estates that lay beyond.

At first, when Edo was only a tiny hamlet on the edge of a marsh, the natives, being poor and without power, were duly impressed by this visible demonstration of power. But the Edokko were a skeptical tribe, and they were likewise proud. They were not the kind to grovel indefinitely without defiance growing in their hearts.

As their city prospered, they grew in both affluence and influence. This was particularly true of the merchants, who waxed wealthy with the profits of trade. In time even the daimyo, impoverished by the showy demands of *sankin kotai,* were compelled to come to these moneyed tycoons for loans to tide them over difficult times. So the Edokko, at first so despised, in time acquired a weapon of their own in money, which they employed cunningly to counter the unpalatable ways of their superiors.

In contrast, the fortunes of the samurai waned. The long Tokugawa peace sapped their martial quality. Without the warlike practice of their profession, they became increasingly soft, venal, and impotent. In fact, some of those in the lower fringes of their class suffered such poverty as to force them to turn commoners altogether.

Thus the tide turned. More and more, as the city prospered and the culture of the townsmen developed and their confidence grew, the odious custom of prostrating themselves before their superiors rankled in every Edokko's heart, coloring his character, stamping the tone of his literature, music, and art. Contemporary Kabuki plays, for instance, are full of situations in which the hated samurai, with their supercilious manner and foppish mien, are roundly worsted by the brusque-but-with-a-heart-of-gold Edokko. The mood expressed in the celebrated play *Sukeroku,* for instance, is only one example of this deep-seated animosity against the oppressors of the common man.

❀

In the story of the rise of the Edokko, his path was not an easy one. He was ceaselessly forced to contend not only with human tyranny but also against many forms of natural calamities, some of them on an awesome scale. His city was repeatedly assailed by fire, drought, famine, earthquake, and typhoon.

A popular saying once described fire as the " flower of Edo," meaning it was a common occurrence and even a point of attraction for the citizens of Edo. When fire broke out, which was often, the good people would rush out in expectation of enjoying the spectacle, all on the assumption that the bigger the fire, the more thrilling the experience of watching it (always provided, however, the burning buildings belonged to someone else.) In the ensuing excitement the crowds pushed and pulled, shins were kicked and noses bloodied, and lusty brawls were not uncommon.

Such wry or pleasurable excitements were for fires of limited dimensions, of course, since all Edokko were aware all too well that fire was their greatest enemy. An elite class of volunteer firefighters, sporting fancy uniforms and constantly on the alert, was always available in Edo. Even at best, however, both their equipment and practices were primitive when measured by modern standards, and their mission was largely limited to preventing the flames from spreading by knocking down buildings with the firehooks and axes that are today so much in evidence in the country's museums.

Edo's first waterworks, one of Japan's earliest engineering feats, was completed in 1654 by the brothers Tamagawa. They laboriously dug a canal from the upper regions of the Tama River to the city's outskirts and carried the water from there to the center of the city by means of open flumes. These, however, were inadequate to provide means for fighting any but the smallest fires, with the result that the " flowers of Edo" blossomed all but unchallenged when a strong wind happened to be blowing toward the most heavily built-up areas.

Edo's most memorable fire occurred in 1657 in the days of the fourth shogun, Ietsuna. On the morning of January 18, a fire broke out in the Maruyama Honmyo-ji, a temple in what is now the Hongo district. For months the city had suffered under a drought that parched buildings and dried up practically all sources of water supply, from wells to moats and river beds. Unluckily for the fated city, a strong wind happened to be blowing vast clouds of red dust that day, fanning the flames and spreading the blaze with incredible rapidity. Sparks leaped across streets and over walls, savagely licking the tinderbox houses of wood and paper.

The doors of a prison at Demma-cho were opened to save its inmates. Further away, the keeper of the town gate at Asakusa received a wild rumor intimating the prisoners were running amok. In one of the most horrifying mistakes of the time, he hastily ordered the gate closed. The fleeing prisoners, augmented by thousands of other townsmen trying frantically to escape the heat, jammed in front of this gate, and there they were roasted alive. Ten thousand bodies were counted on the spot after the fire.

By nightfall of the first day, the fire had invaded Nihombashi. Flames consumed not only the crowded downtown quarters but also the palatial town houses of daimyo to the north and west of the castle. Next day, the blaze spread to Kyobashi, then to Ginza, Shimbashi, and Koji-machi, finally coming to a halt at the water's edge in the bay. The main tower of Edo Castle became a pillar of fire and flames began leaping to the citadel's battlements. In the final reckoning, countless houses, including five hundred mansions belonging to the daimyo, were consumed to ashes and three hundred temples and shrines were destroyed.

In the downtown area where the commoners lived, large stretches were denuded of everything save occasional charred skeletons of the citizens' former homes. The fire continued for two days and two nights until January 20, when the wind at last abated, only to be followed by a heavy snowfall that blanketed everything in white as far as the eye could see. Many people who had escaped the fire, but were made homeless, now froze to death in the blizzard as they huddled outside in the cold. It was estimated that more than 108,000 people died from this double ordeal of fire and snowstorm.

In 1707 a calamity of another kind overtook Edo, terrorizing the populace. On October 4 severe earthquakes shook western Japan. These were followed on November 23 by tremors of sharp intensity around Edo, accompanied by strange underground roars. The earth around Mt. Fuji trembled repeatedly, and the mountain erupted, showering ashes on Edo. Then two days later, at ten o'clock in the morning, the sacred peak shook with a tremendous roar, and smoke spouted above the trees and snow in which the mountain was clad. For the next four hours this once fair mountain was enveloped in writhing smoke. The earth shook; the people were terror-stricken. Excited travelers streamed into Edo with the news that Mt. Fuji was afire. Soon the sky over Edo turned bright red and a steady rain of ashes began once again to fall on the city. For more than two weeks black cinders and gray ashes rained from the sky, darkening the landscape, transforming familiar objects all around into ugly specters.

At night a streak of fire and a column of smoke could be seen in the distant heavens above Mt. Fuji. All traffic along the Tokaido highway was halted. Shrines were crowded with people offering prayers for divine intercession. Even in the middle of the day there was the weird spectacle of people going about carrying lighted lanterns, so dark was Edo under the black haze.

Although the eruption finally stopped on December 9, visible for miles around were charred boulders and rocks as big as fists that had been strewn over the land as if by the hands of a Titan. When the smoke finally cleared, a knoblike protuberance was visible on Fuji's side. It is known to this day as the Hump of Hoei, because the eruption that created it occurred in the fourth year of the Hoei era.

These were only a few of the travails that forged the character of the Edokko. In the face of nature's willful ways, the sorrows of man are many and bitter, but mightier than these is the courage of his spirit. He is a creature of dreams. After each calamity, he starts anew, rebuilding his city with ungrudging toil. Such a man was the Edokko.

We know him quite intimately because of the still-extant Kabuki dramas and the innumerable *ukiyo-e* prints left from his period. Japanese literature abounds with descriptions of him. He was a vivid figure in a vivid age. He was also quite an intriguing fellow. He was spirited, and he was vain.

Unlike his more prudent brother from Osaka, he was a careless fellow, a reckless spender who could never let an evening pass by without spending the last yen in his pocket. He was also something of a dandy, doting on fineries on which he spent a small fortune that he could ill afford. Nourishing his pride with bravado, he scorned to show weakness. Yet for all his brusque exterior, he remained inside a perennial softie. He was a sucker for every sad tale of a brother in need. If you doubt this point, you need only to observe how easily to this day beggars along Ginza milk Tokyoites by displaying sad-eyed puppies in front of them and letting the yen pour into their outstretched hand.

A forthright character, the Edokko detested moodiness and vacillation in any form. He was quick to take offense, quick to forget, and not averse to jumping into a good fight. He was fond of spectacle, gaiety, excitement. He took his pleasures as they came, letting the morrow take care of itself. He was blunt-spoken and sharp-tongued. He loved the geisha, the Kabuki, music, and laughter, and he had a decided weakness for the many fancy dishes that were concocted for his benefit with much culinary ingenuity. He fought bravely, drank heavily, loved well, and dined lustily. Although a witty fellow of some charm, he put great store on face-saving, which he sometimes carried to absurd lengths.

This is the picture we get of the Edokko from examining Edo records. But he is by no means an extinct species. Tokyo's population, as everyone knows, has been vastly increased in recent times by the hordes of outsiders who have poured into the capital from the provinces. This has made the native Edokko something of a rarity, even in Tokyo, but the tradition he bears and the stamp of his character are still all-pervasive. They are the ingredients that make the son of Tokyo today a distinct character, as individual a personage, for instance, as Kyoto's gentleman of culture, or the commerce-minded Osaka man, or the brash, high-postured Kagoshima citizen of the old Shimazu-clan tradition.

Ginza, literally "silver seat," got its name because a silver mint was situated there in feudal times. Ginza is still the pride of modern Edokko. Today, with long rows of willow trees lining its sides, the street is perhaps as well known as Piccadilly or Broadway. Here are the department stores, restaurants, beer halls, night clubs, fashionable jewelers, silk stores, and other emporiums. The back streets of Ginza, a paradise for night life, have more bars, night clubs, dance halls, and eating houses per square yard than any other city in the world.

A fascinating area for the visitor, the Ginza is a jumble of the old and the new, of the West and the East. Gay-colored kimono, representing the East, are seen side by side with the latest creations from Paris or Rome. One may enjoy the scents of Japan's own green tea in one shop, while the place next door may be redolent with the aroma of coffee from Arabia or Brazil. The high twang of the samisen mingles with the music of mambo and rock 'n roll. Here one can enjoy Peking duck, filet mignon, *tempura,* or *sukiyaki*. Or he can feast on *tai* (sea bream) broiled whole, its golden tail raised high on the platter to delight Japan's aristocrats of taste.

Ginza is the home of the great department stores. The biggest and most famous of them all is Mitsukoshi, near Nihombashi some short distance to the north. It is old, and it is a remarkable institution as stores go. As early as 1650 a form of department store flourished around Nihombashi and south toward Ginza.

Operated under the early name of Echigoya, Mitsukoshi thrived with the rise of the commoners. Branches were soon opened in Kyoto and Osaka. This move was a shrewd stroke of business acumen, since it enabled the store to act as broker in transferring funds of wealthy clients from the old imperial capital in Kyoto to the new political center in Edo. This was how the system worked: As the real political rulers of the realm, the successive shogun exacted taxes from the daimyo. Most of these lords had their fiefs in distant places, many in western Japan. Communications between Edo in the east and Kyoto and Osaka in the west were hazardous in those days of bold highwaymen who robbed and pillaged all up and down the Tokaido highway.

To surmount this difficulty, at tax time the western daimyo were in the custom of entrusting their funds to Echigoya for transfer to Edo, 300 miles away to the east. Echigoya at the time was dominated by a resourceful entrepreneur by the name of Mitsui Hachiroemon, who used the money to buy goods in Osaka, which he then sold in Edo. He used the proceeds to pay the shogunate's treasury on behalf of his clients. These transactions he accomplished within sixty days, to the satisfaction of his patrons. Needless to say, he reaped handsome profits for himself in the process.

Under such lucrative conditions, Echigoya prospered and the basis was thus laid for its present-day pre-eminence in the merchandising field. In 1895 the establishment was renamed the Mitsui Dry Goods Store after its founder, but it was not until 1908 that the store got its present name of Mitsukoshi.

Japanese department stores in general are not merely merchandising marts but show places as well. They serve as cultural centers, theaters, art galleries, and music halls, in addition to their function as retail outlets. With skillful showmanship, their operators sponsor art exhibitions, concerts, jumping-frog contests, dog shows, lectures, beauty pageants, and any and all enterprises that seem at the moment capable of drawing the greatest throng and thus, as a by-product, encouraging free spending among their customers, who find the wares displayed en route too desirable to resist.

Most Japanese department stores have traditions going back centuries. Along Ginza, going south from Nihombashi, are first the Mitsukoshi (founded in 1673), then Shirokiya (1663), Maruzen, Takashimaya (1831), Matsuya, Ginza Mitsukoshi, Komatsu, and Matsuzakaya (1707).

A broad avenue, running roughly east and west, crosses Ginza at 4-chome, the dead center of Ginza. Here are the most expensive pieces of real estate in Japan. East on this avenue and thereabouts are located the big movie houses. The imposing Kabuki Theater, rebuilt after the war in its original Japanese style of architecture, is the pride of this district, and so is the Embujo, another legitimate playhouse.

West of 4-chome, and still on the same avenue, is located Sukiyabashi, the Times Square of Tokyo. Here are located the Asahi Shimbun Building, the New Tokyo Beer Hall, and the Nishi Ginza Department Store. An old canal, formerly one of the moats of the Imperial Palace and long a sore spot for civic-minded citizens because of its stagnant waters and foul smell, has happily been eliminated. An elevated expressway now roars above the fill-in, giving a new dimension to this crossroads of Tokyo. Nearby is Yuraku-cho Station, which is flanked by the Sogo Department Store. Beyond Sukiyabashi to the east is Hibiya with its park, the Imperial Hotel, and a colony of fancy movie and revue houses.

Modern Ginza, like the Ginza of old, is still the home of the true Edokko. The fellow has not changed. He still loves the ladies, loves a drink. He is still the fancy dresser he always was. He still loves good food, fine entertainment, and likes to put up a good front. He is a freewheeling, free-spending, argumentative soul who is forever fascinated by the fineries, the raiments, and the thousands of baubles that dazzle his eyes, set there by canny shopkeepers all up and down the Ginza. He entertains lavishly, often beyond his means, forgetting the morrow and the reckoning it brings. Whether he is a plutocrat who dines in style or a humble citizen patronizing a street stall, he dines with the joy, enthusiasm, and taste of a man with three hundred years of Edo culture behind him.

1. Summer fireworks on the Sumida River, Ryogoku Bridge.

Tokyo...

▲ 2

2–4. The Imperial Palace. Near the gate seen in plate 2, and likewise in the snow, Prime Minister Ii Naosuke was assassinated in 1860. Two rings of moats, one partly seen in plate 3, surround the imperial preserve. Sakurada Gate, seen in plate 4, served as main entrance when, before the emperor transferred his court from Kyoto to Tokyo in 1869, the Tokugawa shogunate ruled Japan from this stronghold.

▲ 3

▼ 4

▲ 5

▼ 6

▲ 7

5. Palace Plaza. The fountains commemorate the wedding of the Crown Prince and Princess in 1959.

6. Marunouchi, commerical center of Tokyo, seen beyond the moat of the Imperial Palace.

7. National Diet building. Completed in 1936, after being under construction for eighteen years, the three-storied structure is 215 feet high, the tallest building in Japan. It contains 390 rooms, and accommodates both the House of Councillors and the House of Representatives.

▲ 8

▼ 9

8. Palace gate, framing in the distance the Diet building.

9. Kinryuzan Senso-ji, better known as Kannon Temple, dedicated to the goddess of mercy; Asakusa.

10. Statue of Takamori Saigo, tragic exemplar of the samurai; Ueno Park.

▲ 10

11. Buddhist worshippers in a small temple in the Meguro district.

12–13. Kannon Temple. At the Koro, plate 13, the devout seek miraculous benefit from smoke of incense. The woman at the left brushes her daughter's head with the fumes to imbue her with intelligence.

▲ 12

▼ 13

14.   The approach to Toshogu Shrine in Ueno Park. The stone and bronze lanterns which line the path were the gifts of wealthy daimyo.

15. Ueno's most familiar landmark, the vermilion pagoda of Toshogu. The shrine is dedicated to the memory of Tokugawa Ieyasu and was founded in 1626.

▲16

▼17

16. Gate of the Thunder God, Asakusa. The straight, shop-lined avenue beyond leads directly to Kannon Temple.

17. Nighttime tracing of head-lights at Ginza's 4–chome, one of Tokyo's most famed cross-roads.

18. Nichigeki Theater, Sukiya-bashi. The theater is famous for its elaborate musical revues and, on the upper floors, burlesque and strip shows.

▼ 18

▲ 21

▲ 22

19–23. Kabuki. Plate 19 is a scene from one of the idyllic interludes known as *michiyuki* ; 20 depicts an *oyama*, or female impersonator, applying his make-up; 21–22, also backstage, reveal the highly stylized make-up used in this art form; 23, the "Lion's Dance," is a high point in the Kabuki repertoire, and the goal of all actors.

▼ 23

24. An outdoor image of Kannon, goddess of mercy, extending her benediction over Asakusa.

3

The Titans of
Marunouchi

STANDING OUT LIKE A JEWEL IN A SETTING, the old castle of Edo and its moats are the glory of the city of Tokyo. From whatever direction one approaches them, the first impression is one of agreeable surprise. Driving northward from Yokohama, for instance, one passes through dismal areas of factories, smoke, and ugly houses that are the bane of large cities. Then suddenly, as one approaches Hibiya from the south past Tamura-cho, one comes upon this collection of castle towers, moats, and pine trees that seem to come out of a more stately past to bid him a gracious welcome. This island of beauty inside the busy metropolis is Tokyo's fairest landmark.

Hidden behind stone walls and wooded embankments, the castle was once surrounded by two main sets of moats that were designed in medieval times as double protection against enemy assaults. The moats that survive today are merely remnants of what was once an elaborate system of defenses that consisted of successive rings of moats and canals stretching as far away as Sukiyabashi and beyond.

The moats to the southeast of the castle contain placid pools where reeds and wild herbs grow, forming an invitation to wildlife. Stocked with carp, this whole watery area is in fact a refuge for many varieties of waterfowl that annually migrate from Siberia.

One stretch of the western moat is distinctly Japanese in character but is also in fine harmony with the modern spirit of the metropolis. Both foreigners and Japanese have praised the gentle downward slope extending from the Hanzo Gate near the British Embassy all the way to the Sakurada Gate near the building occupied by the Metropolitan Police Board. Paul Claude, French poet and former ambassador to Japan, was charmed by it, especially in early April when the footpath running along the bank of the moat was magically transformed into a fairyland of cherry blossoms.

The moats on the eastern side across the Imperial Plaza are bounded by Tokyo's busiest and finest boulevard, designated Hibiya-dori or Hibiya Avenue. The most important part of this thoroughfare starts roughly at Tamura-cho near where the national NHK radio studios are located, and ends at Kanda-bashi. Along most of its length, from Hibiya Park to Ote-machi, this broad avenue faces on one side the imperial moats and, on the other, Marunouchi, the heart of Japanese big business.

Some of Tokyo's largest and finest buildings, presenting an impressive face of masonry, glass, and concrete, none over the maximum height of nine stories, rise along this avenue facing the palace. These include the famous Imperial Hotel, designed by the late Frank Lloyd Wright; the Nikkatsu Building; the Daiichi Life Insurance Building, where General MacArthur established his headquarters after the war; the old Imperial Theater; the new Palace

Hotel; and the huge Ote-machi Building, reputed to be the eighth largest office building in the world.

Two blocks east of Hibiya Avenue is Tokyo Station, which is scheduled to be replaced in the near future. Built in 1914, this landmark dominates Marunouchi and recalls the European city scene of half a century ago. It is a low, squat building of vast dimensions spreading out over the city landscape. This desultory spreading is the result of numerous extensions that have been built around it, off and on, all during its career to accommodate the ever-rising flood of traffic that passes through it every day.

The station is busy at all hours, but the crush reaches its peak in the rush hour, when commuting hordes start moving in a tide. The old red-brick building today has a shabby look. Inside it is an entire community in itself, with its own neon lights and glitter. It harbors a maze of passages lined with stores. It has innumerable places catering to shoppers, diners, and pleasure-seekers of all kinds. Here are arcades, restaurants, beauty parlors, barbershops, offices. There are also hotels, a big department store (Daimaru), a public bath, and stock brokerages. A person, if he so chose, could live in comfort inside this sprawling monster for years on end without having to leave its confines.

Of the more dramatic incidents to take place here, the assassinations of prime ministers top the list. First to meet this fate was Satoshi Hara, a champion of the common man, who was stabbed by a fanatical rightist on November 14, 1921. The other was Osachi "The Lion" Hamaguchi. Bushy-maned and leonine, the strong-minded Prime Minister was shot as he emerged from a train one morning in November, 1930. He was rushed to a hospital where, through modern surgery, he was miraculously snatched from death. He lived painfully for a while amid the political uproar that followed the attempt on his life, but finally died of causes attributed to the gunshot.

All around Tokyo Station are the modern buildings of Marunouchi. In them are located the headquarters of the nation's great commercial enterprises. Tokyo is not only the capital but also the center of the nation's industrial empire, whose seat of power reposes mostly in Marunouchi.

❈

For all its secure position today, Marunouchi curiously was a latecomer on the Tokyo scene. In the time of Ieyasu, the spot where Daimaru Department Store now adjoins Tokyo Station was a marsh covered with reeds. As the first shogun reclaimed much of this area around 1603, expanding his castle and guarding it with rings of moats, he also built small houses here for his retainers.

In Edo days, the whole area from the moats to Nihombashi was considered part of the castle itself, hence the name Marunouchi, meaning "inside the circle" of the castle. Rows of warehouses stood here, and one part that remained unoccupied was turned into a parade ground.

After the Meiji Restoration of 1868, both the mansions of the lords and the tenement houses that stood next to the parade ground were vacated. Some of the larger buildings were converted into government offices such as the Justice Ministry and the Supreme Court; others were taken over as barracks for the Imperial Guards.

In those years, Marunouchi reached the nadir of its fortunes. Although neighboring Nihombashi flourished, Marunouchi wasted away like a neglected stepchild. Its once-proud mansions remained tenentless, soon turning into ghostly skeletons. Its deserted streets became filled with tall grass, and pedestrians were often attacked here by robbers in broad daylight.

Then came a change. Unable either to continue the upkeep or raise the necessary funds to rehabilitate Marunouchi, the government in 1890 appealed to private interests to take this white elephant off its hands.

The four leading houses which dominated business in that period were Mitsui, Shibusawa, Okura, and Mitsubishi. The first three regarded the government's plea sourly as an invitation to bankruptcy, but Mitsubishi gambled on Marunouchi's strategic location between Nihombashi's shopping center and the government offices at Kasumigaseki. It acquired this fabulously valuable piece of real estate, now worth untold billions, for a meager million and a half yen. Today it would be impossible to acquire a single *tsubo* (six square feet) of space in Marunouchi for that price. Like the purchase of Manhattan from the Indians for the reputed price of a song and some wampum, the acquisition of Marunouchi by Mitsubishi proved to be one of the luckiest bargains on record.

Mitsubishi had other consideration beside the price in acquiring this land which, in those early days, was dubbed Mitsubishi's Prairie. Its keenest business rival was Mitsui, the trading house which was then spreading wide and handsome in Nihombashi. Mitsubishi was searching for a stronghold of its own, where it could put down roots as a counter to Nihombashi. Marunouchi seemed worth the gamble.

Yataro Iwasaki, who founded the Mitsubishi holdings, was one of the giants in an age of giants. He was a contemporary, in an another land, of Andrew Carnegie. Like his American counterpart, he was of lowly birth. A native of the out-of-the-way island of Shikoku, he started out in a small way. His first interest was shipping, a vital industry for an island people. He early acquired ships, built companies around them, and merged them with other commercial enterprises that he founded until he at last amassed the basis of a vast corporative structure.

In all his dealings, this tough entrepreneur worked hand in glove with the government, since it alone, in the early Meiji era, had the power and controlled the funds necessary for building a modern industrial economy on the slender substructure of the old economy of Edo. A big man physically, he sported a sweeping walrus mustache and Japanese kimono. To strengthen his business position, he entered politics as an ally of Shigenobu Okuma, the liberal prime minister. This tactical move boomeranged, since he became the target of bitter partisan attacks.

When the government, to improve Japan's trading position, formed a subsidized maritime company, Iwasaki gave it such hot competition that the government soon had no choice but to agree to merge it with his own company, forming the Nippon Yusen Kaisha line, which finally broke the virtual foreign monopoly on the profitable Japan-China steamship trade of that early era. Yataro Iwasaki himself died in 1885 shortly before the merger was completed, but by that time he had built up the basis of the Mitsubishi structure to the point where it was readily consolidated into a family holding company soon afterwards under his brother Yanosuke Iwasaki.

All this harks back to the basic post-Restoration policy by which the government itself, anxious to give the country modern industries as quickly as possible, promoted and managed enterprises in the major fields of industrial endeavor and then later, at almost ridiculously low prices, handed them back to a few private companies. This was how Mitsubishi, for instance, acquired the Nagasaki Shipyards, which in 1956, 1957, 1958, 1959, and 1961 built more tonnage of shipping than any other yard in the world.

These are a few examples of the way in which a huge business firm, Mitsubishi, began to expand into a business empire in the middle of the Meiji era, before the turn of century. It eventually became—together with Mitsui, Sumitomo, and Yasuda—one of the four greatest *zaibatsu,* or financial-industrial combines, in Japan.

The *zaibatsu* managed, in time, to control a large proportion of Japanese industry during the decades up to the

Pacific War. They became so powerful in time that the Occupation Forces felt it necessary after the end of the war to try and end both their power and the abuse of it, and the *zaibatsu* were ordered to break themselves up into separate entities as a matter of public policy.

❀

Much has been written about the influence of these mammoth combines that were formerly controlled by a few immensely wealthy families in alliance with the government and the war machine, but more should be told of what happened afterwards. More should be known about the more equitable distribution of wealth that followed the war, and the spread of initiative and free enterprise among the people once these qualities had been freed from the hands of a small group of powerful families.

The postwar growth of the Japanese economy is one of the world's amazing phenomena. The country is enjoying a sports boom of unprecedented proportions in golfing, boating, bowling, mountaineering, swimming, and track. All over the city, office buildings and apartments are sprouting and the city throbs with the pound of pile drivers. Eight hundred thousand cars, trucks, and motorcycles jam the streets where only 59,000 existed before the war. And the death rate from traffic accidents is the highest in the world.

Since World War II Japan has emerged as the first Asian nation to approach Western standards of living. Less than a century after its awakening from feudalism, it ranks today among the world's great industrial powers. Its national output stands near $45,000 million—four times the highest prewar level. Its exports, at almost $5,000 million a year, are more than five times the prewar high.

Japan is, after Canada, the biggest trading partner of the United States. The country ranks fourth in the world in steel production (after the U.S., USSR, and Germany)

63

and launched 2,183,147 tons of shipping in 1962, an increase of 383,000 tons over the previous year. This was twenty-six per cent of the world total for that year, and maintained Japanese dominance in a field where it has been the leader since 1957.

High hopes are centered on the electrical industry, since this may well hold the key to Japan's economic way of life in the coming decade. Thirty-two per cent of the world's radios are produced here, and Japan was second in the world in television production in 1961. In that year one firm, the Matsushita Electric Industrial Company, produced more television sets than any other company in the world. This fact is even more startling when it is noted that a little more than a decade previously not a single set was in existence in the whole country save for a few experimental models.

Popularization of electricity for daily use has transformed national habits. Radio, television, refrigerators, air conditioners, and a hundred other appliances have taken away drudgery and given the people leisure. They have created employment, raised standards of living, and spurred the economy to unprecedented heights of prosperity. As exports, they have helped to balance Japan's international accounts. For years textiles were traditionally the mainstay in Japanese exports. Shipbuilding has come to replace textiles in recent years, but the future may see a new turn in favor of the fast-growing electrical industry.

This industry is dominated by a relatively few giants headed by Hitachi, a $200 million concern and one of the world's great corporations. It manufactures all kinds of products, from tiny transistors to huge generators and locomotives. Tokyo Shibaura Electric (Toshiba) is next in size, followed by Matsushita.

The spiritual father, so to speak, of the Japanese electrical industry was Hiraga Gennai, sometimes called the Japanese Benjamin Franklin. He was a scientist, an experimenter, and an author. He delved into the study of electricity around 1770 from books smuggled into the country from Holland. After experimenting for seven years, he finally completed his "Magic Box." This consisted of a crank, some gears, two chains, and a ball of glass whose friction produced electricity as it whirled around inside the box.

The story goes that this fun-loving inventor, in one of his more playful moods, one day invited thirty pupils of a Buddhist school to join him in an experiment that was promised to give them the thrill of their lifetime. His guests consisted mostly of young acolytes studying for the priesthood, in addition to a few neighborhood girls.

He instructed them to hold hands in a line inside a large chamber in the temple. Innocently and with great expectancy, they all waited for something wonderful to happen. For his part, Gennai returned to an adjoining room after instructing the two boys on each end of the line to hang onto the metal on the sliding door that separated his study from their chamber. As he fastened the chains to the metal on the door and cranked his machine, all bedlam broke loose in the other room, amid squealing and dancing of girls and would-be bonzes. Something shivery had streaked through them, to their amazement.

After the commotion had subsided, Gennai emerged to explain, with a smile, that what he had done was to reproduce the lightning of the sky, and the thing that streamed through their bodies was *erekuteru* (electricity), and not the evil power of the devil they believed it to be. To convince his young charges, he then caused flames to leap from his fingers, and he lighted a saucer of *shochu* (a Japanese liquor) without using fire.

The practical application of electricity came much later in the post-Restoration era, but Hiraga Gennai's sly joke is still remembered.

The heart of big business is in Marunouchi, but it also

sprawls out into neighboring Nihombashi, Ote-machi, and Yuraku-cho. Nihombashi is Japan's Wall Street. It is here that the stock market is located. The other two districts are also important, among other reasons, as the home of journalism—which in Japan is big business. Of the Big Four in this field, each with a multimillion circulation, one is located in Ote-machi and the other three in Yuraku-cho.

The fastest-growing newspaper, though fourth in point of circulation, is *Sankei Shimbun,* located in Ote-machi. It is typical of the others in the manner of its wide-ranging influence through the mass circulation of its publications that find their way into every corner of the land.

Due to the relatively short distances between the great centers of Tokyo and Osaka, on the one hand, and the rest of the country, on the other, these publishing houses leave no room for the small newspapers to compete with them on any but the most insignificant scale. The giants publish their main editions in Tokyo and Osaka, distributing them all over the country by fast trains and planes. For the far-distant hauls such as Hokkaido in the north, they employ facsimile transmission devices so that identical pages made up in Tokyo, for instance, can be turned out practically simultaneously some five hundred miles away in Sapporo.

Sankei's big building in Ote-machi is likewise typical of other headquarters of journalism. It is not merely the home of a financial complex, but constitutes a kind of a cultural center. The Sankei Auditorium housed in the building is used for theatricals, concerts, conventions, and other gatherings. Its smaller assembly hall, designed in the manner of the United Nations Assembly, has a simultaneous translation system, with earphones for each member of the assembly. There are numerous other chambers and places for such activities as art exhibitions, fashion shows, adult education, dining and wining, dealing in stocks, shopping, and a whole host of other activities.

Sankei is not merely a publishing firm; its far-flung activities extend into many diverse fields. Its president,

Shigeo Mizuno, is an influential figure in industry. Besides Sankei, he controls holdings in television, pulp, radio, and other enterprises. His career represents the typical success story of a skillful, energetic operator of free enterprise, Japanese style.

The others of the Big Four newspapers are located in Yuraku-cho, south of Marunouchi. These are *Asahi, Mainichi,* and *Yomiuri.* Unlike *Sankei,* which grew to its present influential stature after the war, their history goes a long way back before the war.

Journalism in Japan is relatively new, as history goes. The pamphlets and pictorial copies that appeared intermittently in Edo were not newspapers in the strict sense. The modern form was invented by a remarkable man, the only Japanese, so far as record exists, who ever talked and shook hands with Lincoln.

On March 12, 1861, Abraham Lincoln's attention was shifted for a moment to something far away from the question of slavery which then plagued his country. On that day he was introduced to Japan, which was then a fantastic feudal society on the other side of the world. The man who told him all about it was a Japanese, the first of his nation to receive a private interview with a president of the United States. He was Hikozo Hamada, known in Baltimore circles as Joseph Heco.

A brilliant linguist and adventurer, he was only twenty-five years old at the time, but already he had behind him ten years of knocking about the world. Although details of his meeting with Lincoln are spare, it is known that Heco was employed at the time by the secretary of state as his official interpreter. It was through this official that Heco was introduced to the President. Lincoln was so impressed by the personality of his Oriental visitor that he introduced him to his Cabinet.

Aside from written evidence, we have a good idea of

how Heco looked when he shook hands with Abe Lincoln. There exists a good likeness of him. The photograph was taken on February 22, 1862, in Baltimore, and he doubtless looked very much like the picture at the time he visited the White House. The picture shows him seated, clasping a cane. He sported a mustache, chin whiskers, and a bow tie. His bobtailed coat, looking a trifle oversized, hung loosely around his long figure. Save for his face, which was on the stern side, his ungainly frame made him look, at first glance, like a smaller Oriental version of Lincoln, and one is inclined to suspect that he had purposely posed in such a way as to enhance this resemblance.

We have considerable information concerning Heco's far-roving career because he turned journalist later in life and wrote nostalgic reminiscences of his early exploits. In late life he became a confidant of Prince Hirobumi Ito, the Meiji-era statesman, who consulted him in drafting the constitution that remained in force in Japan until the present constitution was promulgated after World War II.

The exploits of this remarkable man began with a shipwreck. Hikozo Hamada, as he was then known, was stranded on a desert island off the Japanese coast in 1850. He was then only fourteen years old. He was picked up by an American sailing vessel and desposited in San Francisco, later to be reshipped to Hongkong and Macao. While in Macao, he struck up an acquaintance with a restless State Department employee by the name of Thomas.

Thomas had been hired to interpret for Commodore Perry, who was then preparing his fleet for his famous entry into Japanese waters. Impatient of the long delays that preceded the sailing, the two adventurers, Japanese and American, decided to desert their mission for quick riches in the gold mines of California.

After their surreptitious arrival in San Francisco, the two friends parted company. Thomas went after the gold, but the Japanese went to Baltimore to study English. He soon acquired a ready command of the language. In Baltimore also, he was baptized as a Christian under the name of Joseph Heco. He became naturalized as an American citizen in 1858.

A resourceful person, Joseph Heco was also a persuasive talker. He worked his way into the good graces of William Gwin, the senator from California. Through the lawmaker's influence Heco obtained a commission as a United States naval officer on the U.S.S. *Fenimore Cooper,* a survey ship bound for duty in the Pacific.

The odyssey of Heco, which he wrote himself, makes interesting reading to this day. His diaries are full of amusing observations, gossipy comments, and journalistic accounts of strange places, customs, and people he encountered, with himself as the hero.

All through his wanderings, Heco worked hard for a chance to return to his native Japan. He kept shifting from one ship to another, trying to board one that would take him to Nagasaki. He finally reached that port on June 17, 1859. From there he proceeded to Edo. He ended up by being hired as an interpreter for the American Consulate in Kanagawa through the recommendation of Minister Townsend Harris, whom he had met earlier in Shanghai.

In January of 1860, the *Kanrin Maru* left Edo on its historic voyage across the Pacific, the first Japanese warship ever to cross an ocean. As may be expected, aboard the ship was Joseph Heco. Eventually he found himself back in Washington, where a party of Japanese diplomats signed the first Japanese-American treaty of amity and commerce at the White House in the presence of President James Buchanan. That was in 1860. In the following year, Lincoln was elected president, and shortly thereafter Heco met him in the White House.

Heco's career after 1861 had its high moment when he played an important behind-the-scene role in the drafting of the Japanese constitution, but his star dimmed rapidly thereafter. He worked for a while as an interpreter for the U.S. Consulate in Yokohama. He resigned this position to write a book, the first ever written in English by a Japanese.

While in the United States, Heco had been greatly impressed by the resourcefulness of American newspapermen. Their daily publication of a huge flood of printed matter fascinated him. By contrast, Japanese methods in this field seemed to him fantastically outdated.

By 1866 we find him engaged in a publishing business of his own in Tokyo. Despite his energy and fresh ideas, he was not a success in this field because, by nature, he was ill-equipped to be a businessman. As often happens, his competitors used his ideas and grew fat with profits, while he himself seemed never able to make ends meet. He did, however, make one permanent contribution to the journalistic trade. He invented the word *shimbun* to denote newspaper, a term still in use.

Details of his later years are vague. He died at the age of sixty-one in Tokyo on December 12, 1897, a poor man. Born a Japanese, he died an American. He was buried in a cemetery in Aoyama in Tokyo, where a simple moss-covered tombstone marks his grave. On the face of this stone is inscribed in English the name of Joseph Heco. Underneath are six Japanese characters indicating that this is the tombstone of Joseph Heco.

Nothing is inscribed to indicate that he had spoken with Abraham Lincoln.

4

Shimbashi

Gourmets, Geisha, and Glitter

"SHIMBASHI IS MY TYPE OF WOMAN, COMPLEX, nocturnal, alternately bouncy and sophisticated, lavish and decrepit. Shimbashi is all things to all men. Shimbashi is Montmartre, Greenwich Village, Broadway. Shimbashi is the pulsating concentrate of Tokyo." The Night Owl, a Tokyo newspaperman with a flair for words, describes Shimbashi in this fashion. The assorted charms of this dowdy village in the heart of Tokyo certainly offer their several attractions to her many lovers.

As a geographical entity, Shimbashi lies between Sukiya-bashi to the north and Hamamatsu-cho to the south. The area is full of bars, night clubs, dining places, geisha-houses, and a hundred little shops selling baubles and tinsel and other inexpensive wares.

Shimbashi is a leisurely lady. She is a little seedy and past

71

her prime, it is true, but nevertheless a lady in her own fashion. Take, for instance, the matter of her predilection for the time-honored custom of beauty sleep, though at the wrong side of midnight. She is notoriously a late-riser. Everywhere else, from Marunouchi to Ginza, time is the tyrant, and office workers and shopgirls hustle and bustle to their appointed tasks promptly each morning as if under an invisible whiplash. But not in Shimbashi.

Shimbashi's day does not break until after midmorning. Belatedly, around ten o'clock or later, life begins in the village. Slowly, the debris of the night before is swept away. About this time, too, the shutters that barricade Japanese houses into burglar-proof fortresses begin opening one by one with resounding clacks.

Then the lethargy evaporates. The streets begin humming with traffic. First to feel the quickening of life are the coffeehouses. The brew here is strong, the aroma pungent. Here gather small men of business with something to sell, meeting agents looking for something to buy. Models go into huddles with photographers. Others have other businesses. They may include executives, shopkeepers, cabaret hostesses, as well as impresarios, film directors, novelists, show girls, or just ordinary denizens of the village trying to shake off the fuzziness lingering from the night before.

Shimbashi by daylight has a dilapidated look. She is colorless and bare. She lacks the sparkle, for instance, that distinguishes the Ginza. At night, however, as darkness mercifully veils her dingier aspects and neon signs boast their flamboyant colors, Shimbashi comes into her own. Primped for the night, the village is like a painted strumpet, with the same careless swagger.

Behind Shimbashi's thoroughfares are narrow alleys that wander about, ill-lit and shabby. Although the upper stories of the houses here are ablaze with light, there are pools of darkness below in the back streets where lovers often spend half a night quarreling and making up. The arguments are endless and the lies transparent, but they go through the motions of patching up just the same. They are puppets unable to break free of the strings of compulsion, even when their love, like yesterday's rice, has long since become cold or even tasteless.

Shimbashi's streets are untidy. The debris that collects here is not always the kind that can be swept away with a broom. The ambulant variety is usually found stranded in the cheap bars that abound. Off and on, these frowzy-haired barflies are seen staggering along sidewalks, like harbor boats on a windy day. In fine weather or foul, they flop crazily on the pavement. People walking the narrow ways are forced to make a detour around them. Despite such embarrassments thrust nakedly into their path, none among the careless hearts ever stops to console them.

Other vignettes of life unfold. The nightly intrigues go on in the immemorial manner of men and maids. A sage once said that the love that blooms under the lights is only for the night. He may have had Shimbashi in mind, for here the pursuit of illusion seems to be everybody's business.

Here hope is born, or love dies, or frustrated hearts meet their kind to fashion new lives on the ashes of the old. Here, too, the ineffable ecstasy of youth has its day before the poetry is drowned by cheap liquor and cheaper women.

Behind the curtained windows, and with only a few lights blinking through chinks in the walls, the timeless party goes on. Some night-spots dress their girls in country-type kimono. The girls look deceptively demure, but that is only for effect. Other places wrap their hostesses in plush evening gowns. Although these slant-eyed maids in fine feathers are no chic chicks, their valor is undoubted. There are clubs here specializing in tall girls in high pumps; others insist on busty females wearing cheaters, accenting even further their ample gifts. Still other night-spots project only willowy ladies to attract those who like them slim and fragile.

So the race is on to collect the prettiest girls obtainable, but the more down-at-heel places find the pickings slim, and they end up with leftover maids richer in enthusiasm than physical endowment.

There are so many restaurants and night-spots in Shimbashi, all laid out row on row, block after block, that one wonders how they all can survive the competition. The doubt is dispelled, however, once the night sets in and the hordes of pleasure seekers begin converging. In addition to the food and drink, they come here to buy illusion. Hardpressed office underlings here find surcease from the daily harassments of their office dictators. The henpecked husband, with the aid of a little alcohol under his belt, can flex his imaginary muscles before the professionally complaisant charmers and manage to feel like a man ten feet tall.

In this corner that is a world unto itself, musicians and singers make their headquarters. From here, individually and in groups, they tour night clubs throughout the city, alloting so many minutes or an hour to each place before they move on to the next. They earn their stipends elsewhere, but have their roots here because they like the mood of Shimbashi, the freedom and tolerance. So do the long-haired painters, professional comics, mountebanks, gamblers, frauds, poets, and just plain bums. By the natural process of attraction, the nonconformists and skeptics of the law drift to Shimbashi because it is a haven from prying eyes and nobody asks an embarrassing question.

Here the sundry noises that go under the label of music continue through most of the night. Merrymakers from all over town come here endlessly to celebrate one event or another according to the vagaries of their mood. They come laden with *dempyo* (requisition slips) to pay for the food, the wine, and the geisha (when possible) on their company expense accounts.

Near midnight, a curfew is called, but this is only for establishments with a license for orchestra and dancing. For the rest the night life goes on unabated. Lights are turned low and voices muted behind closed doors, but the blue haze of smoke and the clatter of voices inside bespeak eloquently the doctrine, "Drink and be merry tonight, for tomorrow is another day."

It is about this time, also, that life really comes to its own for the geisha, the aristocrats of Shimbashi.

Gei means "art" and *sha* means "a person." Taken together, *geisha* signifies "talented person." She is a rigidly trained entertainer who lives in a world apart, a throwback to a more elegant past. She is usually gifted, witty, and personable. A girl deficient in any of these qualities is not likely to be a geisha.

For the sake of truth, however, it must be admitted that the quality here ranges from the epitome of grace to vapid vacuity, but the general level is high. Studiously complaisant by training to almost every whim of the patron who pays her bill, the geisha thrives in her particular kind of life of slender income and high living.

This latter circumstance is an anomaly stemming from the fact that hers is an anachronous world in which her expenses, such as those connected with the demands of her *okaasan* (nominal mother), rentals, go-betweens, maids, jin-rikisha, and other fees and tips encountered for each engagement eat up all but a pittance of her substantial earnings.

Geisha entertainment is expensive. It is for people of the level of company executives. A single night's entertainment with geisha might well cost more than an ordinary office worker's salary for a full month or more.

The geisha has an old and honored tradition that goes back to the time of Shizuka Gozen. This spirited lady, known in history as the mistress of the celebrated general Minamoto Yoshitsune, was a *shirobyoshi* (dancer), and she is generally regarded as the spiritual ancestor of the modern geisha. In a twelfth-century episode known to every

Japanese schoolboy, this woman of talent defied her captor Yoritomo, the tyrant of Kamakura. When ordered to perform in his august presence, she risked her life to dance a pantomime of defiance, vowing eternal loyalty to her lover, who was the dictator's mortal enemy (see Chapter 11).

Whenever the subject of geisha crops up, the first image that comes to the mind of a Westerner is Madame Butterfly, but the tragic heroine of Puccini's immortal creation was probably a figment of poetic imagination, not an authentic geisha of real life. The Glover House, now a shrine in Nagasaki for all opera lovers, was actually the home of a Scotsman who came to Japan in 1859; his wife was Japanese, and his home overlooks the bay, but the resemblance to the story of Cho-cho-san and Pinkerton ends at this point.

Luther Long, who wrote the novel from which, through Belasco's dramatization, *Madame Butterfly* eventually emerged, may have had in mind the story of a true-life heroine of Nagasaki who was actually a courtesan of the gay quarters. This was Otaki, the eighteen-year-old whom Philipp van Siebold (1796–1866), the famous Bavarian scientist, married in the early part of the last century (see Chapter 16).

There have been many famous geisha, two of whom may be mentioned here. One was Okichi, who was induced by the shogunate in 1857, near the close of the Edo period, to serve in the household of Townsend Harris, first U.S. consul—later minister—to Japan. He lived in Shimoda for more than a year in almost complete isolation beginning September 3, 1856. Various relics from Gyokusen-ji, the temple where he took up residence, are today maintained in a museum at the nearby temple of Ryosen-ji.

A spirited controversy has developed over whether a romance existed between this girl and the far-sighted diplomat Harris, who was a deeply religious man. Among the Japanese, especially among the people of Shimoda, the trend is all for romance, and an opera has even been written about this lesser-known Japanese butterfly.

In this little footnote to history, Shimoda historians suggest these points: Okichi was by profession a geisha, not a housemaid. She was selected by Japanese officials to serve Harris in his household both because of her accomplishments and her proficiency in household duties. They say she was good-looking. She must have been all of this to have been picked for the job out of so many other attractive girls.

Whether she served in any other capacity over and beyond her household duties is, of course, a moot point. Before he turned diplomat, Harris was a New York businessman. Shimoda's historians who have delved into early records say Okichi was hired by the Bakufu to put Harris in a comfortable mood, with the end in view of easing the difficult treaty negotiations then proceeding between Japan and the United States.

More than a grain of salt should be taken with these views of the good people of Shimoda who, with one eye on the tourist trade, are all for the romance that has become a legend. An Okichi Festival takes place there each year to honor her memory, drawing thousands of visitors.

The story continues that Okichi, for all her devotion to duty as a loyal servant of her country, was later regarded with opprobrium by her own people for having consorted with one of the hated "hairy barbarians." Shunned by society, she died heartbroken after having given up so much for an ungrateful country and a fickle lover.

Is this tale a pure myth or has it some substance of truth? No one knows for certain because the evidence is slim and largely circumstantial. The story must remain a tantalizing enigma until someone turns up with some solid evidence. Whether the tale is truth or fiction, it will probably always remain a part of Shimoda's folklore. In fact, it has already become a legend. The museum at Ryosen-ji contains many articles connected with Okichi, including the palanquin on which she is alleged to have been conveyed to Harris's household.

The Cinderella romance of another geisha is no legend.

She was Oyuki, the Kyoto geisha whom the loving eyes of a dashing New Yorker espied one day back in 1901. This celebrated romance assumed international interest because the man was none other than George Denis Morgan. He was a nephew of the fabulous J. P. Morgan, the man who was the single most powerful financial figure of his time.

The plucky younger Morgan, despite opposition all around, finally came back to Kyoto in 1903 and, in the following year, married his geisha sweetheart and took her back to his country. From geisha to wife in one of the wealthiest families in America was a breath-taking leap, but the heroine lived up to expectations as a good wife and companion to her playboy husband.

The young couple lived together in the United States and at Nice in Southern France, but Morgan, who was not in good health, did not live long. After his death, Oyuki returned to Japan briefly but left again for Nice and her husband's memories. In 1938 she came back to Japan for good. Serene and poised, she celebrated her seventy-eighth birthday in 1959, and then disappeared from the public scene. On May 18, 1963, Morgan Oyuki died of pneumonia at her home in Kyoto.

There is some confusion abroad on a point over which the geisha themselves are understandably sensitive. It has to do with virtue. The Western approach to the geisha ranges from the picture-postcard variety to that held by GI's who were reported, in the early days of the Occupation, as rolling down the Ginza yelling, "We want geesha! We want geesha!"

The business of geisha has to do with art, not selling honey. As in any other profession, the standards of personal integrity vary greatly. They tend to relax in the lower levels, as a rule, where a girl at the fuzzy borderline may well be more than necessarily complaisant with her patrons. Needless to say, the same is true in other fields, and this is in itself no excuse for confusing the profession of the geisha with that of her sisters of fallen grace.

The institution of geisha had its imperial day in the Meiji era more than half a century ago. That was the time when it was fashionable for generals, statesmen, and tycoons of industry to go out with their favorite geisha in tow, and the mistresses they disported themselves with were regarded, by the liberal morality of the time, as something to be worn with their persons, like a satorial accessory.

These men sometimes conferred on matters that involved their nation's destiny—or they started the processes that made or broke financial empires—at tables where these ladies unobtrusively, but graciously, poured rice wine as confidantes and companions to help their patrons arrive at the right judgment. Everyone knew which geisha was attached to what general or cabinet minister, and these "business wives," as distinguished from their legal home-bodies, were regarded as necessary for the success of the men's careers.

Shimbashi is a make-believe world where people buy illusion. It is a place where they pay hard cash for euphoria. In all this pursuit of the immaterial world, the sleek and suave geisha plays her role with fine skill. By training and intuition, she knows how to act in a man's world, having been shrewdly schooled in the ways of a man and his requirements. She is a good listener, and usually a bright conversationalist. She has enough discernment to show, when required, her pride, or anger, or devotion. Other times she can be as playful as a kitten, or bend with grace like a willow in the wind, as the saying goes.

Usually sad are the experiences of a foreigner who comes to acquaint himself with geisha. Across the barrier of language, he is bewildered by their subtle exchanges of wit. Used to the warm throb of Western music, he is left cold by the high twang of the samisen. The poetry of song and all the nostalgic associations that go with it are babble to him. The Japanese dances, especially in the classical category, which is the geisha's pride—these are slow in tempo, and they manifestly do not raise any enthusiasm in him.

Only the sakè tastes good, but imbibing it without the flow of verbal companionship seems to him a waste of time. He may try a few dancing steps with the accommodating lovelies, but the Western mood is simply not there. So he ends the evening feeling a bit sorry for himself—and vastly bored. If he is a newspaperman on the hustle, spending a few days here and a few days there to write all about the culture of Japan, he is likely to record his geisha interlude with bile or, what is even more cruel, with laughter.

And that is how, in many instances, the Western world gets its "close-up view" of the geisha.

The geisha, like the art of *ukiyo-e,* may be a passing institution. She certainly has outlived her best days. She is expensive. The middlemen's take of her earnings is an atrocity. The system needs reforming. She is anachronous in the sense that the relationship between herself and her *okaasan,* who sponsors her and gives her the requisite training, is archaic and feudalistic.

The geisha as an institution is already encountering difficulties as other forms of entertainment prosper, particularly the night clubs, which offer leggy shows, fancy orchestras, dancing, and jazz. In the end, she may survive only in that very limited world of the elite male with the money—and the vanity—to be entertained by these most ego-beguiling ladies in the world.

The geisha are Shimbashi's elite, but their grace is not everywhere reflected in Shimbashi. There are sleazy places, especially under the elevated tracks, where the gin is vile and the noise abominable. But for the most part, Shimbashi has her charm. Depending upon one's point of view, she is coy, fetching, sordid, pretty, mercenary, gay, or wonderfully consoling in moments of a man's frustration.

❋

The night-spots and geisha, of course, are not the only attractions of Shimbashi. The place is also a paradise for gourmets. All kinds of eating places flourish here, from minuscule stands for sakè and *yakitori* (pieces of grilled chicken on a skewer) to substantial edifices dedicated to dining, geisha, and high pleasure.

The story of Japanese cuisine in its more intricate aspects is one of many pleasant surprises. One such surprise has to do with a poison. A choice dish relished especially by urban sophisticates is the *fugu,* or blowfish, which gets its name because of its habit of blowing itself into many times its normal size when in danger as defense against natural enemies. The fish is prepared by experts who adroitly remove the entrails and other poisonous parts under water. Since the margin between poison and exquisite palatability is a narrow one, the sure hand of a seasoned expert is required in its preparation. If the gypsy in your palate demands that you try the rare delicacy, be sure that the eating is done in a reputable dining place.

One can go on almost endlessly describing the Japanese penchant for devising many ingenious ways of preparing succulent dishes. They use chrysanthemum leaves, cucumber blooms, cherry blossoms, the aromatic pine fungus, lotus bulbs, and many other herbs and roots which to the Westerner seem strange as culinary ingredients. The more adventurous visitor may want to try *unagi no kabayaki,* or broiled eels, traditionally eaten in the hot summer months. For most visitors to Japan, the first contact with Japanese cuisine will more likely be with either *tempura* or *sukiyaki.* *Tempura* is shrimp or other fish deep-fried in oil and eaten fresh out of the pan while still hot. *Sukiyaki* needs no introduction, since it is today a popular dish in the West.

All these and many more you will find in Shimbashi. How long is this island of happy Bohemia destined to survive amid Tokyo's boom and bustle? The answer is: not very long. Development projects now under way in nearby Yuraku-cho are an omen of the shape of things to come for Shimbashi. Lured by prospects of fat profits, big business will inevitably step in, and Shimbashi will be turned into one gigantic money-making machine. Modern buildings will replace the frame houses. Urbanity will become extinct, and commercialism will run rife. Everywhere the place will sprout steel, concrete, and glass. The new ingredients will be slickness and modernity, not poetry. Life will be just one mass of uniformity, mediocrity, and insipidity.

Mass-produced wares will attract shoppers with factory-made tastes, but these will be without any appreciation for either character or beauty. Middle-class smugness will reign supreme. Sots and buffoons will give way to frenetic females waving newly bought wares at basement counters. Mass dining places will take the place of the individual shrines of good eating. Empty squeals from empty-headed waitresses will replace the irreplaceable gifts of the geisha. As the traveling troubadors depart one by one, canned music will crop up everywhere, blaring forth jazz for nothing.

Poets and gourmets will vanish, along with crackpots and bums. Tolerance and privacy will be gone. Artists and musicians will flee from this environment of the goldfish bowl. There will be no place for a man, for instance, to cry in his beer without silly stares from silly people, nor any haven for a playwright with beard-stubble four days old to sit down and cook his dreams. There will be no true joy or lust for living. There will be no leisure, but only the frenzy to use up time in a meaningless hurry.

And what will become of the geisha? They will probably trek en masse to a new retreat, but a few may even turn up here—which heaven forbid!—as sleek-stockinged, bare-bosomed gold-diggers in a cabaret.

Thus one more turn of "progress" will be made in this strictly material civilization. Shimbashi as the home of epicures will disappear, but what will never fade is the image in many hearts of this Village of Happy Memories.

5
Diet Hill
Statesmen and Assassins

SOME OF THE MOST DRAMATIC EVENTS OF Japanese history have taken place when Tokyo has been cloaked with snow. It was snowing when the Tairo Ii Naosuke was assassinated in 1860, and also when the Forty-seven Loyal Retainers of Ako slew their enemy Kira Kozuke-nosuke in the celebrated vendetta of December, 1702.

More spectacular than any of these, and perhaps more significant in a historical sense, were the events of February 26, 1936, when elements of the imperial troops rose in armed insurrection. This action also took place in the snow. The coup, though unsuccessful, was part of the long story that began with the Manchurian incident of 1931 and ended with Japan's surrender in 1945 in Tokyo Bay. It took place amid a setting of beauty in what has traditionally been the show place of Tokyo, next to the Imperial Palace.

Southeast of the palace lies Nagata-cho, home of the Diet

and the official residence of the prime minister. Aside from the many relics of historical interest found here, Nagata-cho is rich in scenic charm. It has hills and slopes commanding fine views of the downtown buildings and the great grey ships coming and going in the channels of Tokyo Bay.

If one takes a streetcar running westward from Hibiya Park, one comes to a spot marked Gijido-mae (front of the Diet). The wind-swept hill that rises here overlooks the western moat of the Imperial Palace, where ancient pines raise their gaunt forms along the inner bank. Atop this hill is a small park dedicated to the memory of the late Yukio Ozaki, known to his compatriots as the father of Japan's parliamentary system. A great man of peace and a sworn enemy of militarism, Ozaki is best known to Americans for a gift he made to their country while he was mayor of Tokyo more than half a century ago. It was he who presented the cherry trees whose lovely blossoms in springtime attract thousands of sight-seers to the shores of the Tidal Basin in Washington, D.C.

The centerpiece of Ozaki Park is a campanile, a triangular pencil-slender shaft with a dial high overhead on each of its facades. Three times a day chimes donated by the Swiss Watchmakers League sound through the neighborhood, reminding the lawmakers sitting in the nearby parliament of their obligation to the cause of peace to which Yukio Ozaki had dedicated himself.

Nearby is the Memorial Building, where a likeness of Ozaki in the evening of his long life stands on a pedestal, with a cane in one hand and waving his hat with the other. The statue is characteristic of the man. Physically he was a small person, but his casual appearance was deceptive. Within his spare form there stirred a fiery spirit which expressed itself with rare eloquence when as an old man he courageously condemned the conduct of Japanese militarists during World War II.

Ozaki Park stands on the former estate of Ii Naosuke,

whose assassination we have already mentioned. During World War II, the place was the headquarters of the Army General Staff. Its subsequent transformation to a garden of peace was a fine gesture reflecting the country's new peaceful outlook after the war.

The most conspicuous landmark of Nagata-cho is the National Diet, close to the Ozaki memorial. Though unkind critics have described the Diet building as a glorified imitation of Western folly, it has its dramatic aspects. The granite tower and the stately columns over the front steps are Grecian in style. The building not only displays a sense of massive strength but also has the clean lines and eloquent simplicity that are the priceless heritage of the classical Hellenes.

Outside the Diet's front gate is a small plaza. It was here that student radicals, converging in wildly zigzagging snake columns, clashed with the police in 1960 in demonstrations against the revised U.S.-Japan Security Treaty, leading to the cancellation of President Eisenhower's trip to Japan.

Close by the Diet is the official residence of the prime minister. This gloomy two-story building enclosed by a high stone wall has been the setting of many a historic decision in peace and war. Not the least of the events to occur here, in a dramatic sense, was the murder of the prime minister by a gang of assassins in 1932.

The prime minister today has at his service both the official residence where he entertains at small functions and an office building across the street where he attends to state duties. For more elaborate receptions for official guests he uses the Geihinkan guest house near Meguro.

Down the road from the prime minister's residence, on the west side, is a deep gully at the foot of which stand two buildings, one new and the other old. The new one is the recently completed Hilton Hotel, and the other is the Hie Shrine, an ancient edifice at the top of a slope to which access is gained by a long stone stairway.

Hie Jinja, as the shrine is more familiarly known, dates back to the Kamakura era centuries ago. At one time it stood near Edo Castle. It was in that period that this holy abode of gods won particular renown because of an incident which occurred there.

The seventeenth-century episode revolved around the person of Lady Kasuga no Tsubone, wet nurse to the baby who later came to be known in history as Iemitsu the Magnificent. As a child Iemitsu suffered from a near-fatal case of smallpox. At a critical moment during his illness, the fond matron repeatedly made lonely pilgrimages to this shrine, offering to give up her own life to the gods if only they would spare the child, who now seemed doomed with high fever in the ancient castle.

The gods heard her prayer. Both the child's life and her own were spared. The boy eventually grew up to become the powerful third ruler of his dynasty, and he is today best remembered for the dazzling mausoleum he erected at Nikko honoring the memory of his grandfather Ieyasu, founder of the line.

Next to Hie Shrine is the Sanno Hotel, which achieved sudden notoriety when rebels in the insurrection of 1936 made it their headquarters. As we go down the hill from here, we approach the Toranomon (Gate of the Tiger) district, site of the U.S. Embassy.

Wheeling at a right angle northward from Toranomon, we come to the long line of buildings that house the various ministries. This is the heart of Kasumigaseki, home of both the government's executive and judicial branches. Beyond this civilian command post of the nation is the headquarters building of the Metropolitan Police.

We have now completed our little journey around an area roughly horseshoe in shape, which is the seat of government. Its outer bounds stretch from Gijido-mae to the Diet building, the prime minister's residence, the Sanno Hotel,

Toranomon, Kasumigaseki, and the Metropolitan Police headquarters. This also was the line of occupation for the insurgents who suddenly, on the snowy morning of February 26, 1936, moved against the government in a precipitate reach for power for themselves and glory for their country.

❁

The revolt was finely timed. Quickly, as the city began to awaken at the break of day, armed troops formed a cordon around Nagata-cho and Kasumigaseki. Other conspirators, young and determined, spread out to predetermined objectives. They were organized into small mobile task forces charged with specific missions.

Their first objective was to eliminate the government's source of power as a prelude to takeover. Acting coldly, like insentient robots, they assassinated liberal leaders one by one. Among their victims was Finance Minister Korekiyo Takahashi, a rotund octogenarian who looked and acted like the laughing god of good luck, Hotei. Immensely popular with the people, he had begun life in a humble way. He once served as a chore boy for an American family in Oakland, California, in the 1870's. In subsequent years, he rose to become prime minister, although he was finance minister at the time of his death. Also killed were General Jotaro Watanabe, Inspector General of Military Education, and Admiral Makoto Saito, Lord Keeper of the Privy Seal.

Because of a breakdown in communications arising out of the insurrection, foreign correspondents were isolated in the Imperial Hotel, but the earliest reports to reach them told of Takahashi's demise. A friend, it was reported, had rushed to Takahashi's home and found the body of the financial wizard lying on the floor of the bedroom. It was riddled with thirty-two machine gun bullets.

Other rebels moved to the official residence of the

prime minister. Although the ringleaders had planned meticulously, miscalculations occurred. Subordinate troops fumbled badly. The men who were dispatched to assassinate the prime minister, for instance, killed his secretary instead through mistaken identity. Prime Minister Okada, an admiral, had hidden himself in a clothes closet, and thus survived.

Other rebels stormed into the home of Grand Chamberlain Kantaro Suzuki. Upon entering his room, they shot him down without a word. They had been ordered to shoot first without speaking, lest an exchange of words with their intended victim should arouse sentiments that might cause them to falter in the execution of their mission. Though gravely wounded, the old admiral eventually recovered. Nine years later, when an even greater crisis confronted the nation, the old statesman headed the government which negotiated his country's surrender in World War II.

The rebels planned to occupy the War Ministry, the headquarters of the army General Staff, the national Diet, and the official residence of the prime minister. Boldly, the conspirators had planned to force War Minister Kawashima at gun-point to obtain for them imperial sanction of their cause under martial law.

In this extraordinary crisis, the War Ministry was in desperate confusion. Officials were completely at a loss. Finally, at three o'clock that afternoon, a mysterious War Ministry order appeared, without any basis of legality, intimating that both the high command and the emperor condoned the resistance.

Belatedly, the Cabinet met the following day and Tokyo was put under martial law, but there was no immediate disposition to put down the insurrection. On February 28, however, a drastic change took place. There was indignation at the outrages committed against government leaders, and finally an imperial rescript was issued, commanding the men to return to their quarters at once.

During the crisis the government generals wavered. Their counsels were divided. Some secretly sympathized with the rebels. Confusion was so rife among officials that order never trickled down from the nominal leaders of the military to those particular lower echelon officers who led the insurrection.

Finally, on February 29, contingents of loyal troops were summoned from outside Tokyo. They converged on the capital in full battle dress. Their grey helmets and black cartridge belts glistened as they piled out of trucks, their rifles over their shoulders. Behind them, tanks and artillery rumbled though the streets. Long marching columns of marines sloshed through the melting snow, giving welcome assurance to the populace. As loyal artillerymen set up guns in the woods of Hibiya Park opposite the Imperial Hotel, curious onlookers noted that the muzzles were pointed directly at the rebel-seized Diet building just ahead, looming big and clear and seemingly near enough to touch.

The loyalists went about their tasks methodically. As they did so, loudspeakers from tanks on the ground and planes overhead repeatedly broadcast the emperor's command ordering the rebels to return to their barracks. The whole area rained with leaflets containing the same message. All this time, two lines of soldiers, one loyal and the other insurgent, grimly faced each other across the street in the heart of Tokyo. For a while, the cold war looked as if it might erupt at any moment into a bloody massacre.

Abruptly, however, after a tense day, the rebels finally faced up to painful reality. Confronted by grim loyalists with their superior force and reserve power, the rebels now knew that they were defeated. In one group after another, solemnly and in silence, they began returning to their barracks. Their footsteps fell slowly, wearily, as if treading painfully upon a fallen dream. The misled troopers were all young conscripts, many hardly out of their teens. Some had tears in their eyes, others looked straight ahead, their faces completely blank. Behind the mask, however, was a pride that would not permit them, as heirs to the samurai tradition, to show any sign of weakness in the face of failure and inglorious defeat.

First Lieutenant Shiro Nakano, one of the ringleaders, committed suicide. Other conspirators were arrested by officers of the War Ministry. Including non-military participants, about fourteen hundred men took part in this abortive coup. Captain Kiyosada Koda and sixteen junior officers, plus a number of civilians, were tried for sedition and found guilty.

Probing the anatomy of sedition is a difficult task because each conspirator is a world unto himself. There was, however, a common denominator among those who plotted the uprising. They were all addicted to a monstrous sentimentality. They were dreamers of the old imperialist days. They were heady with the glory of the Meiji period. In the end, this fixation sealed their doom.

Among the ringleaders, Asaichi Isobe is best remembered because he was the most articulate. Bespectacled and handsome, he was a physically impressive man. He was big and tall, and displayed the confident air of a leader. In addition, he had literary pretensions of a sort. Although what he wrote gushed with sentimentality, the outline of the man emerged unmistakably clear in the deluge of his outpourings. While his fellows were contemptuous of death, Isobe in turn was contemptuous of this very posture, which he regarded as an earmark of vanity. He disliked the thought of dying. He said so. He regarded the wish for death as a confession of moral bankruptcy.

Each in his own way, the rebels' attitude toward life differed, but the march of justice rolled solemnly on as fifteen officers in three groups were executed at the Yoyogi Military Prison on July 12, 1936. Isobe was in a cell at Yoyogi when rifle shots rang out from the firing squad.

90

He had just finished his breakfast when he heard the traditional *banzai* cheer, which he subsequently described as
the melancholy last voice of the condemned men. A man
with a poetical flourish, he called it the mirthless laughter
that is always found at the end of tears.

There was drama also when another group of rebels,
Isobe included, faced the firing squad a year later. The
day was August 19. It was a clear day, a bit hot, and the prison ground was already set in order for the last act of the
drama. On the way to the scaffold, Mitsugi Nishida, one of
the rebel leaders, talked to his friend Kazuteru Kita, who
was also about to be executed. Nishida asked Kita if they
should give three *banzai* for the emperor before they died.

Kita, it is said, paused a moment for reflection. Already
blindfolded for the execution, this rebel leader declared
softly, in a disillusioned tone, that he did not wish to give the
customary *banzai*.

Squatting on the scaffold, he then thanked the prison
warden for the little acts of consideration tendered him while
he was a prisoner there. Kita's last words were said to be,
"I'm glad I'm permitted to die sitting. It's not good to
die upright like Christ and Sakurasogo [a medieval Japanese
peasant martyr]." As soon as he uttered these words, Kita
and his fellows in treason died in a hail of bullets from the
firing squad.

There was an ironical twist to this story of futility.
Though the participants were defeated as individuals,
their aim to obliterate moderate opinion in the government
and create a military dictatorship received an unexpected
boost by their action. The net result of the February Incident
was to enable the army, which received the credit for suppressing the rebellion, to fasten its grip more tightly upon the
nation than ever before. After the incident no civilian officials dared oppose the militarists publicly.

Today, after nearly three decades, it is not difficult to

see why the plot misfired. The rebels misjudged the temper of a people who were in no mood for a reign of militarist terror. More decisive than this, in a practical sense, was the rebels' miscalculation of the extent of sympathy to their cause within the army itself. The top generals had ideas of their own, more devious and sophisticated, and their views by no means coincided with the brash ideals which the fanatics attempted to foist upon the nation.

In the final analysis, the plot failed because the young insurgents possessed neither the gift nor the training needed to carry a revolution through to a successful end. Amateurs and visionaries, they had no practical program to carry out after achieving their first limited objectives. And most significant of all, the rebels suffered from an inherent weakness which in the end proved fatal: the emperor was not on their side.

❀

The rebellion of 1936 was only one of many internal acts of violence which took place in the unruly decade of the thirties. Among the earliest of these was the Five-One-Five Incident of 1932, which derives its name from the date on which it occurred, May 15.

The violent blood bath that ensued during this two-hour reign of terror was climaxed by the murder of the prime minister. The rebels, all wearing uniforms, also threw hand grenades and fired shots at such places as the headquarters of the Seiyukai Party, the residence of the Lord Keeper of the Privy Seal, the Mitsui Bank, and the Metropolitan Police building.

The tragic figure who stood out in this episode was a man of immense courage, who was also a veteran of countless battles in his long carrer as parliamentarian and political leader. His name was Tsuyoshi Inukai, leader of his party and prime minister of his country. His people knew him best from the many photographs of him that appeared in the newspapers, which depicted him as a small man with a white beard who attended ceremonial functions wearing a morning coat two sizes too large and carrying a cane absurdly long for his tiny stature. In his oversized silk topper and black ties, Inukai was a heaven-sent gift to newspaper cartoonists.

Despite his odd appearance, however, there dwelt in the man a razor-sharp mind and a tongue as keen as a rapier. He was a tough, roaring orator in the old style. He possessed a gift for repartee, particularly in the rough give-and-take of parliamentary debate. His wit was fabulous.

The last moments of Inukai's life were fraught with drama, like something out of Kabuki. There was the same futile confrontation of will against will, climaxed by the final dissolution of his body in an orgy of blood. Or again, his fated life makes us think of a puppet in one of Chikamatsu's plays. The circumstances which finally destroyed him were beyond his control; the role he had assumed in life foredoomed him to extinction. And when the end came, he died as bravely as any samurai out of Japan's storied past.

Putting together the best available evidence, it is possible to reconstruct almost exactly what took place inside the gloomy mansion of the prime minister at about five-thirty on the evening of May 15, 1932. The day had been unseaonably hot. Dressed in a comfortable kimono, Inukai was standing in a corridor in front of the dining room. He was anticipating a hearty supper with his grandchildren and his daughter-in-law. The latter was the wife of his son Takeshi, who was elsewhere at the time. The Prime Minister's own wife was also absent, having departed earlier to attend a wedding dinner.

As the little group waited for supper, they suddenly heard strange noises outside and Fujita, the Prime Minister's bodyguard, suddenly came rushing in.

"Mr. Prime Minister!" he shouted excitedly. "You must go away at once. Gangsters have broken in."

Inukai's daughter-in-law tried to persuade him to flee instantly, but the old man refused to budge. He said decisively, "I shall not go away. I'll see those fellows."

The killers poured into the hallway, searching the rooms one by one, until they abruptly came face to face with the Prime Minister himself. Without warning, one of them shot at Inukai, but the gun misfired. The Prime Minister, unruffled, slowly moved his hand up and down as if to calm the excited intruders. A veteran of many a political battle, he knew how to treat hecklers and ruffians, and he now employed the same tactics upon the men who had come to assassinate him.

"Wait a moment," he urged. "There'll be plenty of time to shoot if you want to. First let's go over there and hear your story."

Inukai led the intruders to the reception room, apparently to draw them away from the small dining room where his grandchildren yet remained. Other members of the family had come to the old man's side during the disturbance, including his daughter-in-law, the guard Fujita, and the fiercely loyal maid Teru, a veteran of long service with the family. In the stereotyped manner of gangsters, however, the intruders motioned these others aside with their guns and then fell in behind the Prime Minister as, arms crossed within his kimono sleeves, he led them quickly away from the vicinity of the dining room. Inukai appeared exceedingly calm. It seemed as if he were merely leading some guests to a nearby room.

A family physician, Dr. Ono, happened to be present in the house at that time, waiting for the opportunity to give the Prime Minister a medical examination. Having heard the commotion at the front gate, he too made an appearance. Seeing Inukai behaving in so nonchalant a manner, the doctor concluded that the uniformed rebels crowding behind the Prime Minister were loyal troops which had been sent to protect the old man from the rowdies outside.

It took the Prime Minister only a few seconds to reach the reception room. As he entered it, the rebels followed closely behind. Precisely at the moment the last of them stepped across the room's threshold, another gang of four men, also in uniform, burst upon the scene from the direction of the back entrance.

One of them shouted, "Shoot!"

A deafening roar of gunshot shook the chamber, and the assassins rushed outside in great haste, leaving their fallen victim behind.

The maid Teru rushed into the reception room. She found the old man, with both elbows leaning on the table, remaining perfectly still. Blood was streaming down his forehead and cheek. He faced Teru slowly and said, "Light my cigarette." The cigarette was already soggy with blood. As she recalled later, she was so horrified by what had taken place that she experienced difficulty in lighting the cigarette.

The Prime Minister's next words astounded her. Though he was obviously at death's door, with blood gushing from his mortal wound, the grand old man of politics said to her, " Bring back those young fellows. I'll talk to them so they'll understand."

Dr. Ono, who had also rushed into the room, asked the Prime Minister a professional question. In reply, the wounded man pointed to his temple.

"This place went bang," he said. "Has anything happened to it?"

Teru unashamedly lied. "The bullet has missed the vital parts, Mr. Prime Minister," she said in her usual booming voice. " Everything will be all right."

But the gallant veteran, full of courage to the last moment, was unable to fulfill his wish to "talk to the young fellows so they'll understand." At ten o'clock that night he vomited blood copiously, passing away while still in a coma at half-past eleven the same night.

There was something big about Inukai's character, something grand in the best liberal tradition of the stout-hearted parliamentarian. Ironically, however, whatever gods ruled the destiny of a Japanese statesman had already loaded the dice against him, and he actually had no chance for survival that evening as he faced the remorseless, insensitive robots who slew him with a single shot of gunfire.

6
Nihombashi
Carefree Days
of the Floating World

AN INVETERATE EDO-AGE TRAVELER WHO WAS
also a magnificent landscape painter pondered one day, a
little more than a century ago, about how to portray the
majesty of a mountain that rose above the Kanto Plain.
That mountain, of course, was Fuji. The more he thought
about the matter, the more he wanted to capture on paper
the beauty of this lovely vision that looked down from far
away upon his favorite bridge.

When he finally completed his picture, he had set down
a lively scene of crowds moving in the foreground on the
bridge, which was covered with snow. Here he put down
peddlers, tradesmen, and cart pullers at work. Here also
were bearers of palanquins and a man of means riding a
horse, attended by a groom. On the river, boatmen in straw
raincoats poled their craft on water as smooth as glass.

This artist with an acute eye for detail was also a master of contrast. He set this colorful throng against the lonely grandeur of winter on the plain. Above all, he placed Mt. Fuji where it properly belonged as the dominating element, brooding majestically over this famous bridge in the heart of the nation.

Such is the scene of Hiroshige's famous wood-block print of Nihom-bashi in the old castle town of Edo, the city which was renamed Tokyo in 1868. There is a modern footnote to this depiction. A story has it that a New England spinster from Boston way stood on Nihom-bashi a few years ago with a book on Hiroshige in her hand. Oblivious of the clanging trolleys and roaring motorcars all about her, she kept asking a stranger who had befriended her, "Where is Fuji-yama? I can't see Fuji-yama."

Doubtless the story is apocryphal, but the fact is that travelers to this day do come to Nihom-bashi with the intention of viewing Mt. Fuji as portrayed in the numerous *ukiyo-e* prints that were sketched from this vantage point in old Edo times. Sad to relate, modern changes have wrought havoc to this traditional view. Buildings of steel and concrete, rising all around, have raised a curtain blocking out forever this particular view of Fuji that once inspired some of the greatest *ukiyo-e* artists.

Nihombashi is the name of both the bridge and the district surrounding it. As a fishing hamlet in the period before the shogun Ieyasu, Nihombashi had probably existed from time before history under sundry different names. As a bridge, its career started with Ieyasu, who built the first span here in 1603.

The present structure, the thirteenth such span built at this identical spot, was completed in 1911 in the last full year of the reign of Emperor Meiji. Upon the succession of Emperor Taisho the following year, the bridge was officially designated the starting point for measuring all roads emanating from this central hub of the nation.

More important than the bridge itself, with its quaint post-Edwardian decorations, is the district which surrounds it. Although physically a prosaic quarter, it is a place of great historic interest. In its days of glory two centuries ago, it was the seat of a brilliant culture. Today, as it was in the Meiji era, Nihombashi is still the center of Japan's financial empire, although in certain other respects it has long since been overshadowed by its more aggressive rivals, Ginza and Marunouchi.

Without any doubt, Nihombashi is still the Wall Street of Japan. Its financial tradition goes back to the days of Ieyasu, who began minting gold coins on the spot where the Bank of Japan now stands. Silver coins were minted further south, at Ginza. The Bank of Japan, first established by the government near the Sumida River in 1882, was moved to its present Nihombashi site in 1896. The Mitsui Bank, oldest in Japan, was opened here for business in 1876, setting a pattern for other banking houses.

When the Mitsubishi organization expanded its enterprises in Marunouchi, Mitsui cornered a section of Nihombashi and ruled a commercial empire that was later broken up by the Allied Occupation after the last war. The old *zaibatsu,* as most students of Japanese finance will recall, were led by Mitsui and Mitsubishi interests and at one time dominated a good portion of the nation's economy.

Nihombashi is the home not only of the Tokyo Stock Exchange but also of the nation's powerful brokerage houses, headed by the Big Four securities (Yamaichi, Nomura, Daiwa, and Nikko). These giants among private enterprises exert enormous influence on the nation's exchanges. They have offices in almost every city and town in the country, where people of all stations, from small salaried men to rich tycoons, buy a share of the nation's wealth in the current wave of prosperity.

It was here, in the heart of Nihombashi, that the great speculators of the past, both in history and fiction, made or lost fortunes at the turn of a ticker tape. Nihombashi, for instance, was the stamping ground of Gyu-chan (Mr. Bull), the hero of an immensely popular novel of a few years ago. *Oban,* as the novel is called, relates the changing fortunes of this physically rotund speculator who not only made and lost fortunes but also won and lost a lady's love in the process.

Written by Shishi Bunroku, this richly humorous work, which later was made into a lucrative movie, gives an absorbing account of how a free-wheeling speculator operated in and around Nihombashi. The novel's interest is heightened by the fact that Gyu-chan is modeled after an actual stock manipulator who lives to this day, ruefully looking back on his experiences with the enigmatic ways and tantrums of the stock market.

Needless to say, the Japanese stock exchanges are now carefully regulated to restrict excesses harmful to the public interest. The government keeps a watchful eye on the exchanges' behavior. Human nature being what it is, however, fortunes are still won or lost by persons who are willing to risk much to gain more.

The nation's major banking firms have made Nihombashi their seat of power, all within the confines of this crowded quarter where an odorous little stream by the name of Nihombashi River flows. The big insurance companies are also located here, and so are some of biggest industrial enterprises, which from this central location direct their activities through a maze of subsidiaries that reach out to every corner of the land.

❀

When Ieyasu visited Edo for the first time in 1590, he found in the general area of Nihombashi a village of some one hundred straw-thatched houses strung along the edge of a marsh. An astute general, he at once recognized the strategic importance of Edo. Its location at the head of

Tokyo Bay and at the mouth of the Sumida River not only indicated the makings of an excellent port, but the castle built here earlier by his predecessors provided a stronghold from which he could dominate the whole Kanto Plain.

When Ieyasu finally received this largely empty land of eastern Japan as his fief, his mind was already set on establishing his capital here. He was a thrifty man by nature. He was also a canny leader who knew what measures to take for survival. His first task was to rebuild the old castle, not only as a military stronghold but also as the visible symbol of political power. He planned the castle as a demonstration of his might, a means by which to impress the warring clans of his district.

Moreover, Ieyasu undertook vast additional public works, even to the extent of directing an army of workers to level the hills around Kanda and fill in the marshes around downtown Edo. He improved all roads converging on Nihombashi. Old records indicate that he paid particular attention to building up that portion of the old Tokaido highway which extended between Nihombashi and Shinagawa, an area which today embraces all of Ginza.

In 1602, a fire destroyed most of Edo, enabling Ieyasu to lay down the present basic outline of the city: the castle of the shogun surrounded by moats, the main business section at Nihombashi, the park at Ueno, and the commoners' amusement center at Asakusa.

Under the shogun's patronage, the city developed rapidly. Only twenty years after Ieyasu established Edo as his capital, the population had increased to 150,000. By 1700 more than a half million people lived here, and by 1887 the number was well over a million and a quarter.

Edo grew not only in physical size but also in the quality of its culture. Within a century after Ieyasu, it had taken primacy over Kyoto as the nation's pacemaker. By the Genroku era (1688–1704), Edo had reached its golden age. The rise of Edo's townsmen was accompanied by a liberal outpouring of talent and a renewed interest in learning. Literature flourished, drama reached a new high level which has never since been surpassed, and the unique art form of the masses had its beginnings here in the famed wood-block prints, called *ukiyo-e* or "pictures of the floating world" because they depicted the lusty, buoyant life of the day.

As the home of Edo's newly-risen townsmen, Nihombashi served as the fountainhead of this revival. Unlike previous epochs, when emperors and generals and the great regional lords were the great patrons of the arts, patronage was now shared with the commoners. Thus the new culture had a broad base. Painting, for instance, had previously been encouraged by a handful of lords and their intimates high in their castle retreats, but now *ukiyo-e* art, as a result of the new wood-block printing process, circulated in every by-street of the town, bringing a touch of artistic beauty into the lives of even the humblest commoners.

The real patrons of art in this period were the wealthy merchants. They had money, they had influence, and they were boundlessly optimistic. As true Edokko, they were lavish spenders, giving free rein to their taste for luxury. They dined on fine foods, clothed themselves in fine raiments, and collected rare works of art. Their aesthetic tastes were at a high level, as yet unspoiled by the decadence that gradually corrupted artistic standards in later days. This happy circumstance of wealth and leisure, and the willingness to savor life over and beyond their former subsistence level, encouraged the emergence of a new class of artists, some of them of a very high order.

Three great men of culture of the Genroku era were the poet Matsuo Basho, the novelist Ihara Saikaku, and the playwright Chikamatsu Monzaemon.

Born of humble parents in what is now Mie prefecture, Basho (1644–1694) experienced a turning point in his life when his lord, who was also his playmate and companion, died when the poet was in his twenty-third year. Grief-stricken by this loss, Basho wandered about Kyoto and elsewhere until he finally reached Edo. There he set himself up as a teacher of poetry, and soon found himself acquiring pupils.

One of these students was a prosperous fish purveyor to the shogun who owned a fish pond east of Nihombashi in what is now Fukagawa. There, on the water's edge, Basho built himself a hermitage. Soon his fame spread from this little hut under a banana tree, and here Japan's greatest poet composed some of his finest works.

Basho's poems are noteworthy for their extreme economy of language, for the images they evoke and the emotions they inspire, all within the confines of the starkly simple seventeen-syllable poetic form known as *haiku*.

Saikaku (1642–1693), who describes the world of the merchant class in the great cities, was born in Osaka. He was thus an Osaka man, but in a broad sense he was part of the great culture of Edo which dominated the land all through the three hundred years of the Tokugawa age. Among his more famous works are *The Man Who Spent His Life at Love-Making, Five Women Who Loved Love, How to Get Along in the World,* and *Eternal Storehouse of Japan.*

Chikamatsu Monzaemon (1653–1724) also was not an Edo man. But, even though he resided in Kyoto, his creative genius was a dominant influence in the development of Edo culture. Chikamatsu breathed new life into Kabuki, the dramatic form which achieved its finest flowering in Edo.

Legend says that a shrine maiden named Okuni introduced Kabuki near the end of the seventeenth century. In those days the river Kamo in the city of Kyoto was a gathering place for light entertainment during the nights of the dry summer season. The sundry performers who flocked there included Okuni, who had abandoned the sacred precincts of the Taisha Shrine in Izumo to seek her fortune in the ancient capital. There she became a favorite attraction, dancing on a platform erected in the river bed.

In a bid to increase her drawing power among the crowds

who flocked to watch her art, this resourceful young woman added supporting roles to her show and some witty dialogue to her repertoire of dances. Thus was born the first crude outlines of what later came to be known as Kabuki, the Japanese classical drama which won many admirers when performed in the United States in 1960.

After Okuni, so the story goes, her art was continued by her sundry sisters of the trade who also engaged in another, far older, profession during after-hours. This caused the city fathers to intervene on moral grounds, with the result that female performers were finally eliminated altogether and Kabuki came to be performed entirely by male actors. The tradition of *oyama,* those male actors who to this day play all female roles, arose out of these circumstances.

From the beginning, Kabuki proved to be a robust art arising out of the popular desire for entertainment. It was earthy, lusty, and plebeian. Successive men of wit, technicians, actors, and showmen added improvisations of all sorts to pull in the crowds. They were an ingenious lot. They invented the revolving stage, the stage elevator, the drop curtain. They devised the runway that brought actors right in the midst of the audience, giving the fans a close-up view of their favorite performers. They added refinements to the techniques of simulation, whether in dueling, seduction, murder, renunciation, or revenge. They produced dances of great polish and style. They perfected Kabuki's broad gestures.

As the Genroku era approached, Kabuki was at that stage of evolution where its audience demanded materials of good quality, and Chikamatsu filled the bill. Thus this man, often termed the Shakespeare of Japan, was both the creator and product of the Japanese theater's golden age.

Strictly speaking, Chikamatsu began his career writing scripts for the puppet theater called *ningyo shibai* (see Chapter 14). He wrote *joruri,* a poetic form of dialogue and descriptive narration chanted to the accompaniment of the samisen in a manner reminiscent of the West's medieval ballad singers. While the chanters recited, the puppets strutted and fought on a miniature stage like real people. Chikamatsu's magic lines made the wooden figures come alive with all the strength and frailty of man, whether in pride, anger, love, hatred, or sorrow.

Chikamatsu's greatest contribution lies in his *sewamono* (play of contemporary society), portraying the world of the common people, rather than that of lords and nobles and great warriors. While he had a precedent in the selection of this theme in the ancient comic plays called *kyogen,* he brought this genre to a new high level of art, giving it depth through a deep sense of compassion and a keen understanding of human motives. Chikamatsu was a master in the portrayal of passion; in the treatment of the double suicides of passion called *shinju* he was without peer, delving skillfully into the dark, complex psychology of this form of self-destruction, which was not uncommon in the time of Edo and later.

Chikamatsu was a sensitive genius with an awareness of tragedy. His plays are full of verve, poetry, and high drama. His lovers are gallant souls, fated but brave, who go to their death together believing in an after-life, convinced that they will gain the happiness denied them in this life. So successful were these plays, originally written for the puppet theater, that they were taken over by the live theater. Thus began the happy association of Kabuki with its greatest benefactor.

Life in Nihombashi in the heyday of Kabuki during and after Genroku had its exciting moments, especially at show time. At dawn each day drums would beat mournfully for nearly an hour, calling forth citizens to take part in the sundry attractions billed for the day. As daylight broke, customers in their holiday finery blossomed out to form ticket lines that snaked through the narrow back streets. Gaily colored banners with announcements brushed in bold characters rose like sentinels along the theater fronts.

Crowds gaped round these gaudy posters emblazoned with the pictures of matinee idols.

The mood was gay. Tickets were inexpensive. The motley crowds, ranging from humble artisans to affluent merchants and their womenfolk attired in silk and satin, trooped in to enjoy a world of make-believe in performances that lasted from dawn to dusk. Because of fire hazards, night performances were prohibited. Even under such precautions, fires destroyed the frame playhouses with ruinous frequency.

We have a fairly complete picture of the life and times of Edo largely because of the unique Japanese art form of the period. This was the *ukiyo-e,* sometimes called *nishiki-e* (brocade pictures). A popular art, usually printed in elegant colors, in their times these wood-block prints served the purposes, in a rough way, of today's Sunday pictorials, calendar art, and pin-ups. Thousands of them flooded the shops and street stalls and eventually found their way into the homes of all classes of townsmen. They treated all manner of contemporary subjects.

The pictures which here concern us most, however, are those depicting Edo's theater at the time of its finest flowering. Called actor pictures, these were the works of scores— even hundreds—of craftsmen, most of whom were hacks, but some of whom emerged as artists of rare skill. In fact, all the famous practitioners of the *ukiyo-e* art produced actor portraits at one time or another in their careers, for it was impossible to ignore the glamor and importance which the stage had assumed in the life of the people.

These and scores of lesser craftsmen toiled long hours in the back streets around showhouses, in and around Nihombashi, presenting us with lively pictures of the actors, the theaters, and the crowds that milled within and without, in all their noisy exuberance. Fighting for survival in a fiercely competitive occupation, these print makers would invade the backstage to sketch the actors as they prepared for rehearsal, and they would then rush off again, working all night, to strike off an edition in time for the next day's performance.

Since Edokko were a demonstrative people accustomed to voicing their likes and dislikes in no uncertain terms, the theater was often rocked by boisterous demonstrations of enthusiasm, sometimes hostile, sometimes favorable, always fiercely partisan. The more wealthy patrons brought their families with them, dining and wining in the boxes while the performances went on. Others, in the tolerant morality of the time, brought along their mistresses instead of wives, drinking repeated toasts to the performers and to the health of the painted and perfumed companions who poured their liquor.

Amid this carefree world of wit and banter, they would suddenly awaken to the gong of temple bell or the soul-striking clap of *hyoshigi* (wooden clappers), reminding one and all of the dark tragedy impending on the stage.

While the Kabuki was the main attraction of the Edokko in downtown Edo, the aristocrats of uptown who lived around the castle enjoyed another form of diversion. This was the Noh, a performance combining elements of dancing, singing, and dramatic plot. Behind their expressive Noh masks, actors moved gracefully in gorgeous robes. Slow in movement, the pantomime was rich in nuance. The stage was small and almost bare except for the simplest of properties. Its back wall, of fine wood, was painted with a stylized pine tree, opulent with color.

In contrast to Kabuki's realism and melodrama, Noh was sternly restrained. By subtle movements and gestures, it stressed the drama of the human mind rather than physical movements. Yet for all this noble restraint, some pieces were exciting to behold, and full of pathos and drama. Some three-hundred pieces are extant today in the Noh repertoire, and they are performed to the chanting accompaniment of *utai* music. Some are mere phantasies, with ghosts and goblins as protagonists; others are simple tales narrated in idyllic settings. In the plays appear court nobles, warriors, peasants, fishermen, monks, and strange demons of the nether world.

A perennially popular Noh piece is *Dojoji*. This is a story of passion in which a spurned maid pursues her priest-lover to a temple in Kii, where he has hidden himself from her under a huge bronze bell. Smouldering with the rage and desire that is known only to a woman scorned, she turns into a dragon for vengeance, wrapping the bell in her coils and melting it with the fire of her passion. On the stage, she first appears as a comely damsel in distress, but later changes into the fiery serpent, and as such she performs the mad dance, a memorable high point in Noh repertoire.

Dojoji to this day is played in both Kabuki and Noh versions. Nihombashi, in the center of old Edo, knew them both, as well as many other performances ranging from the tragic dance of the *Sumidagawa* to the epic of *Chushingura*.

Nihombashi is no longer the spirited hub of Japan's capital, and little remains here today to remind the visitor of the vital culture of the Edokko which flourished some two centuries ago. To the east of Nihombashi, however, where the Sumida River flows into Tokyo Bay, there is an island which is one of the Edokko's few last stands. This is Tsukuda-jima, a tiny, closely-knit community which is a throwback to the Edo period. Its dialect and customs are fragrant with memories of Edo. The place has been spared from both fires and earthquakes that have periodically reduced other spots in the capital. Its buildings are old, its shrines have remained intact since the age of daimyo and samurai, and its annual water festival is one of the picturesque events of contemporary Tokyo.

25. Noh mask of a woman.

Tokyo (cont.)...

▲ 26

26–28. Geisha arriving at a party in Akasaka, which together with Shimbashi is the locale where today these women of long and often influential history play their role in small and exclusive restaurants.

▼ 28

▲ 29

▼ 30

29. A woman vaudeville entertainer, accompanying herself on the samisen, recites an epic tale of old Japan.

30. Dolls made with chrysanthemums appear in the autumn exhibitions. This one represents Sukeroku, a gallant figure in Kabuki drama.

31. Jinrikisha in front of a Shimbashi restaurant. Now these vehicles are used almost exclusively by geisha.

▼ 31

▲ 32

▼ 33

32. Sumida River. Fed by the snows of the Chichibu Mountains, this historic stream is continually contributing to the natural filling-in of Tokyo Bay by the deposit of alluvial soil.

33. Auctioning of tuna at the wholesale market in Tsukiji, facing Tokyo Bay.

34. Tokyo lumberman. He wears a uniform which is a throwback to the Edo period.

35. Farmwoman from Miyake-jima, a tiny island which, though 105 miles south of Tokyo, is embraced by the city's metropolitan jurisdiction.

▲ 34

▲ 35

▲ 36

▲ 37

36. These elderly Japanese women wear the sober colors which tradition prescribes for their age.

37. "Strong men" at a festival in Asakusa, Tokyo's most popular amusement section.

38. Asakusa's Dragon Festival, held twice yearly, in March and October.

39. Annual water festival at Tsukuda-jima, the island at the mouth of the Sumida River which still preserves many of the manners and appearances of the Edo era.

39 ▶

40. Bodhidharma, a Buddhist saint of India and China, is reputed to have sat in meditation for such a long period of time that his arms and legs withered away. He is the subject of innumerable Japanese toys, such as these *daruma* dolls.

▲ 41

41. Toy drums and comic masks.

42. Paper carp, symbol of perseverance, are flown above housetops on the day of the Boys' Festival, May 5.

43. Rush-hour crowd at the ticket gate of one of Tokyo's tram stations.

▲ 42

▼ 43

▲ 44

▲ 45

▼ 46

▲ 47

44. Customers at a street stall selling *yakitori*, grilled chicken.

45. *Sushi*, raw fish on cold rice with a touch of horseradish and dipped in sauce—one of Japan's unique culinary delicacies.

46. Cheap food stands abound in the city, this one under the railway in Shimbashi.

47. Innumerable small streets consisting of nothing but bars and restaurants come into their own at night in Tokyo.

48. Around New Year's Day, Tokyo's firemen don ancient costumes and perform acrobatic feats reminiscent of the skill and agility for which the firefighters of old Edo were famous.

7

Ueno

Samurai's End

THE FEMALE BEAR CUB SHYLY RETREATED
to a corner of her cage the day she was presented to the
village school. By next morning, however, the plump little
foundling made friends with the school children. They
named her Koma-chan. A frisky pet with an instinctive
wisdom of her own, she soon learned to beg for tidbits by
standing on her hind legs, her forepaws held out before her
in a comic suppliant manner. She loved swimming, and she
could climb trees with the agility of a monkey.

The happy days of summer came and went in the north
country of Akita, and then the first snow began to fall.
One morning the children found that the furry orphan had
crawled into the corner of her cage, appearing cold and
lethargic. This was a sign that she was ready for her first
hibernation. As there was no place in the tiny village suitable as a resting place for her long winter sleep, the villagers
decided to send her to Ueno Zoo.

To the keepers at the zoo in Tokyo, the experience of Koma-chan is nothing unusual. Creatures of the wild, both young and adults, are continually sent there by owners who find themselves unable to give them the care they require.

Juro Hayashi, the zoo's superintendent, is a champion of all kinds of nature's children, from the great white heron to the giant salamander, Japan's most unusual creature. A tender-hearted man dedicated to animal welfare, he is kept busy responding to calls for sheltering wounded swans, orphaned deer, sick boars, and even the rare wild antelopes that occasionally stray from their mountain fastnesses in the Japan Alps.

While the zoo is Ueno's star attraction, accounting for the largest number of visitors, it is by no means the only one. Here in Tokyo's most spacious park, covering an area of 210 acres, are located all manner of cultural institutions ranging from museums and art galleries to shrines and temples. Ueno is also rich in such places for recreation as playgrounds, swimming pools, and tennis courts.

Of particular interest to art lovers is the Museum of Western Art which is situated near Ueno Station and houses the famous collection of the late Kojiro Matsukata. This playboy industrialist, who was the son of former Prime Minister Masayoshi Matsukata, had a particular fondness for impressionist paintings of ninteenth-century France and for the sculptures of Auguste Rodin. His hobby turned out to be his country's great good fortune, because his treasures have been donated to the state and can now be seen in this museum designed by the celebrated French architect Le Corbusier. A shipping magnate in the period of World War I, Matsukata was a collector with a mind and a manner all his own. He bought his treasures in characteristic fashion by wholesale lots, blocking out with a wave of his cane whole sections of exhibited masterpieces he wanted to acquire.

All the great French impressionists are represented here, including Monet, Manet, Pissaro, Renoir, Gaugin, Cezanne, Van Gogh, and Degas. These are augmented by some very interesting works by painters of the preceding period such as Courbet, Millet, and Delacroix. The museum also possesses the largest collection of Rodin sculptures in the world.

North of Ueno's Shinobazu Lake lies a series of stone steps that climb up the hill to the Toshogu Shrine, where some of the bones of the shogun Ieyasu are buried. Within these compounds is the familiar five-story pagoda, which appears especially lovely in springtime surrounded by the cherry blossoms that abound in this whole area. In front of the temple runs a tree-shaded avenue, both sides lined with massive stone and bronze lanterns that were donated by the wealthy daimyo of the Tokugawa period.

Toshogu's main gate, called Kara-mon (Chinese Gate), is of particular renown. On its two sides stands a set of four dragons carved in wood. These are the masterworks of "left-handed" Jingoro, Japan's fabulous sculptor whose better-known figure of the sleeping cat can be seen at Nikko. While still a boy, so the story goes, Jingoro once drew the likeness of a mouse so skillfully that the family cat pounced upon it, thinking it alive. In 1625 the second shogun, Hidetada, planned to build a Buddhist temple called Kanei-ji, in Ueno. He summoned all the great architects, artists, and artisans of the time for the task. Jingoro was among them. He labored night and day with fantastic energy, and in twenty days he completed his masterwork—two dragons leaping upward toward heaven, and two plunging down to the sea. Though finished in the rough-carved style of his liking, the serpents seemed so alive that their fame soon spread throughout the land.

Then one morning, so the legend says, the dragons were found to be dripping with water. Morning after morning this inexplicable phenomenon continued, until a witness was found who testified that the fiery-looking creatures, in the dark of night, had been in the custom of going to nearby Shinobazu Lake to bathe. Upon hearing this report the officials ordered that a metal mesh be made to cover the panels where the dragons were located, and forever afterwards, so it is said, the wayward creatures never again wandered away for their nightly ablution.

The wooden dragons have since been moved to their present site by the Kara-mon, where to this day they can still be seen behind wire netting. In point of fact, the present mesh replacing the original nets is a modern device employed to guard against careless handling by visitors, but the carvings are genuine. Though sadly scarred by time, they still seem strangely alive, still instinct with their original smouldering ferocity. They have been designated as national treasures by a panel of expert antiquarians.

At the end of the Toshogu's avenue of lanterns is a monument dedicated to General Ulysses S. Grant, onetime American president, who visited Japan in 1879 with Mrs. Grant. Further to the south is Kiyomizu-do temple, the subject of a famous *ukiyo-e* print by Hiroshige. Kanei-ji, the traditional place of worship of the successive Tokugawa shogun, is located in the extreme northern part of the park, and within its quiet precincts is the mausoleum of the Tokugawa family, which ruled Japan all through the Edo period.

Less familiar, but equally interesting, is another of Ueno's relics. This is the *chashitsu,* or tea-room, located in back of the National Museum. Known as Rokuso-an (Six-window Sanctuary), this ancient edifice was built nearly 350 years years ago by Kanamori Munekazu, a master of tea ritual. It was originally located in the Kofuku-ji, a temple in Nara, but was moved to Tokyo in the Meiji era. Built of wood and thatch, it is a humble creation, but it has priceless worth because it is one of the very few authentic *chashitsu* which have been preserved in their original form. It symbolizes, in a sternly simple fashion, a way of life that revolved around the classical cult of tea ceremony, with its doctrine of asceticism, self-discipline, and other-worldliness.

On the park's southern extremity are Ueno Station, starting point for all trains to northeast Japan, and the busy Ueno shopping district with its Matsuzakaya Department Store and a myriad other shops catering to lower-middle-class shoppers. This region constitutes the front gate of Ueno Park, and the most conspicuous landmark here is the large statue of Takamori Saigo, one of the most tragic heroes of modern Japan. The career of this statesman reached its culmination with the Meiji Restoration, when his soldierly personality proved outstanding even in the brilliant company of other notable figures who together ushered in the modern era for Japan.

The statue of Saigo overlooks the spot where a bitter last-ditch battle was waged between the forces he led under the imperial banner and the diehards of the old shogunate in the War of Restoration. It was a battle fought with courage on both sides, but it was also the most futile engagement in Japanese history.

So peaceful now are the sunny hills of Ueno that one can hardly imagine the awful carnage that occurred here less than one hundred years ago. Except on Sundays and holidays, the battleground is today a place of quiet charm. It abounds in monuments and places of historic interest. Here on a green bank lies the azalea garden commemorating the wedding of the Crown Prince and Princess in 1959, and here also stand the cypress and magnolia trees which General and Mrs. Grant planted as mementoes of their visit to Japan. There are green vales here, and tree-lined slopes, and family groups can be seen on sunny days enjoying picnics on the lawn. And over this whole region rises the Toshogu's vermilion pagoda, an image of tranquillity dedicated to the memory of Ieyasu, who started Tokyo on its road to greatness.

For all this picture of peace and well-being, this was the spot where the soil was dyed red with the blood of men who died in one of the most hopeless battles ever fought. All things considered, it was a needless slaughter, because the men who fought so valiantly under the banner of the last shogun actually never had a chance of victory. They were so outnumbered and outequipped by the modernized loyalist army that their desperate action as faithful retainers of their lord Yoshinobu was only a gesture, noteworthy more for its gallantry than for any effect it had on the course of history. The tragedy of these men was complete because they died defending a cause which had already been decided months before by the "abdication" of Yoshinobu, the last in the long dynasty of Tokugawa rulers. For this story of the willful men who defied reason for honor, we must go back to the events that led to the revolution of 1868 and the turning point of modern Japan.

Despite some controversy over details as to what actually caused the downfall of the shogunate, the basic outline is quite clear. Confidence in the military dictatorship of the Bakufu had been undermined by the intrusion of foreign warships into Japanese waters and ports that had been sealed to foreigners for centuries. This face-damaging situation for the shogunate was aggravated by other factors, particularly foreign bombardment of Japanese fortresses.

Internally there was the eroding of the shogunate's powers through economic change brought on by the growth of a merchant capitalist class. An anachronistic feudalism could not survive in the emerging industrial world, but the Bakufu, under Yoshinobu and his predecessors, was unable to make the transition with enough dignity to satisfy the proud young men of Japan's western clans, who turned to the emperor as a rallying point in seeking a new deal for their country.

The triumph of the imperial cause in the end was due, in the main, to the political cunning and foresight of some very able leaders. Mostly young men below the ministerial rank, these destined leaders of their country came from the clans of Satsuma, Choshu, Tosa, and Hizen, and worked in collaboration with a number of Kyoto nobles and Osaka merchant families. They were fierce zealots, determined and dedicated.

The crux of the matter was that the Bakufu, confronted by superior foreign forces equipped with guns and warships, was unable to resist the foreign demands for concessions. To the loyalists, who gathered in Kyoto, this was national humiliation. Raising the standard of the fifteen-year-old Emperor Meiji, who had succeeded to the throne, they girded themselves to overthrow the shogunate.

The shogun at the time was Yoshinobu, a peaceable and reasonable man. Although he had the support of fanatically loyal men who were willing to fight for him, he wisely chose to "restore" administrative powers to the emperor and thus save the nation from a bloody conflict. He made this decision in response to a memorandum from the Lord of Tosa in November of 1867, urging him to restore governing powers into the hands of the sovereign so that a foundation might be established on which the country could take her stand as the equal of other countries.

Yoshinobu, it was evident, was in no mood to fight to preserve his regime, but his overzealous henchmen carried the day. Determined to punish those whom they regarded as the upstarts around the throne, they attacked the loyalist forces in January, 1868, some three weeks after the proclamation of the restoration of full powers to the emperor. Despite their numerical superiority, the attackers were beaten at Toba and Fushimi, both near Kyoto. The defeat was due to the defection of important elements to the enemy at a critical juncture in the battles.

Yoshinobu, who had been in Osaka Castle at the time,

fled to Edo by warship. After a short stay in Edo Castle, he instructed his military advisers to negotiate a peaceful surrender of administrative powers with the representatives of the emperor. Then he retired to the Kanei-ji, the temple in Ueno.

Meanwhile, the loyalists marched on Edo—the city was not renamed Tokyo until later in the year—in three columns and from three directions. They were headed by Prince Arisugawa as nominal commander in chief, but the actual military operation was in the hands of Takamori Saigo, head of the Satsuma clan, who had a reputation as a godlike leader of peerless valor and widsom. He and Rintaro Katsu, the ex-shogun's adviser, soon came to a complete understanding regarding the transfer of powers from the old shogunate to the new government under the emperor.

All this, it would seem, was enough to convince any rational mind that further bloodshed would serve no useful purpose, but the ways of men in a time of tension and mixed loyalties are often inscrutably devious. There were many who believed that the shogun, once he was induced to give up his prerogatives, should be given a place of honor in the new government. However, the young zealots of the anti-Bakufu alliance, particularly the men of the Satsuma and Choshu clans who dominated their cause, had other ideas. They were comparatively young, intolerant, and full of fight. They were determined to strip the house of the shogun not only of its powers but also of its material possessions. This, of course, produced violent reactions among certain men loyal to Yoshinobu. It was part of their code of loyalty not to submit tamely to what they regarded as a usurpation of power by the western clans who were out to overthrow a regime which had ruled the country ever since Ieyasu in 1600.

Some fifty men who formed the inner core of Yoshinobu's retainers set up headquarters in a temple in Asakusa, vowing to resist the new regime. Other men quickly flocked to join the forces of the Shogitai, or Corps of Justice, as they called themselves. Since the place was too small to accommodate all volunteers, the headquarters was moved to Ueno, and the man chosen to lead them was Hachiro Amano.

Even as the rebel leader took command, the transfer of Edo Castle to the imperial forces took place peacefully on April 11. In the meanwhile, the ex-shogun Yoshinobu, guarded by two hundred men of his household, left Ueno for Mito, the traditional home of the Tokugawa family. As his faithful vassals, the men of the Shogitai also sought to accompany him as a bodyguard, but the request was refused.

At this moment of mounting anger, sorrow, and bewilderment among the men of the Shogitai, an ecclesiastical officer of the Kanei-ji stirred them with misgivings. His name was Kaku-o In Gikan. He openly charged that the ambitious clansmen of Satsuma, Choshu, Tosa, and Hizen, using the youthful emperor as a "front," had conspired to seize power for themselves from the legitimate Bakufu, and that their charge that the ex-shogun was a national traitor was an utter falsehood. The true disturbers of the country were the men of these four clans, he told them. He further declared that all men loyal to the Bakufu must unite to destroy the "real traitors."

Even before these inflammatory words were uttered, the men of the Shogitai had been baffled by the surrender of their lord's castle and the sudden end to their way of life as the shogun's retainers. Now they began to gird themselves for resistance against the new regime.

In calculated sorties, they collected firearms and ammunition, killing and injuring loyalist soldiers in the process. This was clearly a rebellion, and there was no illusion on either side as to its true significance. General Saigo, a man of large character, tried at first to ignore the Shogitai's recalcitrance, but he could not remain indifferent for long. Moreover, an officer of the Saga clan by the name of Eto Shimpei was so incensed by this state of affairs in Edo that he communicated the fact of the Shogitai's rebellion directly to the imperial court in Kyoto. Gravely concerned over this new turn of events, the government in Kyoto at once dispatched General Masujiro Omura, an expert in Western military science, to assist Saigo in suppressing the insurrection.

The battle began on May 15. Rain, which had begun the previous night, was still falling as dawn broke. Shinobazu Lake overflowed into all nearby roads, forcing troops on both sides to fight in knee-deep water.

General Omura ordered the loyalists to bombard all enemy positions on Ueno Hill, which was already surrounded by double lines of his own infantrymen. His artillerymen, equipped with the latest Armstrong field guns imported from England, wrought havoc in this preparatory bombardment.

Further south, at a spot near where the Saigo statue now stands, Hachiro Amano took command of the rebel forces, and he then realized for the first time the demoralizing effectiveness of the loyalist firepower. Accompanied by his staff officers, he quickly withdrew to nearby Shinobazu Lake, where his own field pieces, hidden in a cavelike shrine of the Fox God, began firing back.

Troops of both sides fought savagely all day on the muddy roads around the lake and in nearby hills. In a reckless assault, the desperate rebels finally broke through the loyalists' advance position and began to attack the enemy's main defenses.

The rain fell that day intermittently. It was a wet, dreary, blustery day.

The rebel forces, who had entrenched themselves at the Kanei-ji, meanwhile erected an outpost consisting of piles of furniture and *tatami* mats collected from nearby temples and homes. The loyalists picked a contingent of Satsuma men to smash this point of resistance, but the attackers were repulsed with heavy losses. Their mission was made doubly

134

difficult by the fact that the defenders had emplaced a field gun on a hillock at Sannodai just above the outpost and had begun firing at the enemy at pointblank range.

To stop these harrassing tactics, the loyalists hauled their own cannon up to the second story of a restaurant at Yamashita and began firing on the rebel's gun emplacement, wrecking their batteries and scattering the men manning them. Finally troops from the Satsuma and Higo clans smashed through the Black Gate and into the temple. There, at close quarters, both sides wielded their samurai swords in a fiercely fought battle.

As the afternoon waned, the battle seesawed furiously without a decision. General Omura, who was in the west tower of Edo Castle as General Saigo's chief operational officer, issued an order instructing his men to win a decision by nightfall. He gave this instruction while he stood viewing the woods of Ueno through a field glass. A statue of him in this pose now stands on top of Kudan-zaka behind Edo Castle, now the Imperial Palace.

Just as General Omura had instructed, by nightfall the woods of Ueno turned into a ball of flame and the men of the Shogitai were annihilated.

Yoshinobu lived for many years afterwards. With the passage of time the bitterness that prevailed between his partisans and the men of the new regime gradually healed, but it was not until 1902, some thirty-four years later, that Emperor Meiji received him in audience. Soon afterwards this last ruling descendant of Ieyasu was raised to the rank of prince, the highest in the nobility.

The career of General Saigo had another kind of ending. For his services as one of the handful of brilliant men who effected the Restoration, he was made a field marshal and also became a Sangi, or High Councillor, equivalent to a present-day Cabinet minister. Despite such honors, trouble began brewing for him which was to make him one of the tragic figures of history.

Soon after the Restoration, leaders of the new government replacing the old Bakufu became badly divided over the question of Korea. Saigo led the faction demanding strong action in a dispute that rose with that hermit kingdom over its refusal to recognize the new post-Restoration government in Tokyo. In essence, Saigo wanted to apply to Korea what may be termed the Perry treatment, endeavoring to open Korea's door by force, if necessary. In this he was overruled by the faction which wanted to build up the country on a firmer foundation before undertaking adventures abroad. Arguments between the two sides were heated and prolonged, and in the end Saigo and his supporters withdrew from the government.

Saigo is generally regarded today as the flower of the samurai—courageous in adversity and magnanimous in victory. He possessed a magnetic personality that attracted fanatically loyal followers everywhere, and his great name has since become a legend.

For all his soldier's virtues, however, as a statesman Saigo was on unequal terms with his more sophisticated opponents in the government. While he remained all his life in his island realm, men like Tomomi Iwakura, Toshimichi Okubo, and Hirobumi Ito, who advocated a more cautious course, had knowledge of life abroad, and knew from first-hand experience the enormous strides which the Western nations had achieved, in contrast to the relatively shaky position of their own country, which was only then casting aside its outmoded feudal structure. These men expressed forebodings that any embroilment in a war against Korea would inevitably bring Japan into an open conflict with the Western powers, and they were not sufficiently confident of Japan's position to risk such a test of strength.

The men who opposed Saigo's views had what may be termed the realistic modern approach, while the brave man of Satsuma remained to the end the symbol of sword-wielding samurai in an age of guns and warships.

After leaving Tokyo for his home province of Satsuma in Kyushu, Saigo established a school which was devoted chiefly to training in the martial arts. Young men from all over Kyushu flocked to his classes. He became an idol to all the malcontents of the nation's samurai class who, since the Restoration, had been divested of their class privileges when the government abolished the country's feudal institutions. Eventually, in 1877, armed rebellion broke out in Satsuma with Saigo at its head.

The campaign, which lasted for several months, was a bloody affair. Saigo's army was made up of members of the old samurai order. The government, on the other hand, used a new conscript force consisting of men of all classes in the belief that commoners, when properly trained and indoctrinated, could fight as bravely and as effectively as any class of elite professionals.

At first, fortune smiled on Saigo's cause. At the head of a force of thirteen thousand men, he easily took Kagoshima. After consolidating his base there, he led his men northward on March 15 to meet the enemy at Kumamoto. Everywhere they advanced, they were hailed by the populace as heroes, and fresh volunteers flocked to join his army. It was a heady moment for Saigo. By the time he reached the north, his army had more than doubled in size to some thirty thousand men.

Kumamoto Castle, built in the early seventeenth century by Kato Kiyomasa, was now guarded by a garrison of only five hundred men under Tateki Tani. But this fortress, engineered in the time of Ieyasu, had been so skillfully built that its massive walls proved impregnable against Saigo's cannonade.

While the beleaguered men fought for time, a large government force under Prince Arisugawa hurriedly left Osaka to come to their aid. Ironically, he was the same man under whom Saigo had fought their common enemy in the earlier War of Restoration.

At Tabara-zaka, a hill north of the castle, the imperial forces and Saigo's men clashed in battle. Both sides fought furiously up and down the steep slope in hand-to-hand combat with swords. Prince Arisugawa, who could afford to keep back fresh reserves, used them judiciously to relieve his tired men as the battle raged through the day and night, and this strategy proved decisive. Saigo's men suffered a major defeat on this occasion chiefly because they lacked reserves to counter their enemy's fresh troops.

After the battle of Tabara-zaka, Saigo's forces dwindled rapidly as he vainly sought to retrieve his waning fortune in repeated stands all along the long road southward to his home province of Satsuma. By the time he made his last stand at Shiroyama in Kagoshima some months later, his once-proud army of 30,000 had been reduced to only 3,700 men.

There, late one September afternoon, the imperial forces opened up an artillery barrage against his positions. Near sundown, after having bade farewell to his men in a dugout which served as his headquarters, Saigo left for a ravine in the battlefield. He was accompanied by his closest friend Shinsuke Beppu. Although instinct told him that his cause was now beyond recovery, the battered but unbowed commander, ill with fever and weary from lack of sleep, comported himself in style to the last. He rode the short distance in a sedan chair borne by bearers.

Just as Saigo alighted from the archaic conveyance, a stray bullet struck him in the abdomen, and the big man toppled heavily to the ground, mortally wounded.

It was apparent that his last moment had come. As he looked back on his eventful career, Saigo must have found no solace. His victories in the earlier War of Restoration were now ten years behind. Most of his friends who had fought with him in that war were either dead or fighting against him now. Except for a bare handful, his comrades in his present cause had been killed. Among his closest friends, only Beppu was left. There are no records of what the two said to each in the gathering gloom of that dark little ravine on the side of the hill near which the Kagoshima railway station today stands. What actually took place, however, is plain enough from the evidence. Saigo asked Beppu to take his life by decapitation in the samurai manner, since he did not want to fall into the hands of the enemy. It was the only course for a Satsuma warrior to take. Regretfully, and with sadness, his best friend complied. Beppu then hid the severed head under a stone bridge to keep it out of the hands of the enemy.

All this, of course, sounds somewhat like a scene out of a Kabuki melodrama, but it is an episode that actually took place at nightfall on that fateful September 24 of the year 1877.

Having disposed of Saigo's head, Beppu returned to battle. As his last act on earth, he hurled himself at the enemy shouting, "The great teacher is dead!" and there he fell before enemy fire just as he had planned to do. The handful of Satsuma men who remained in this lost cause all committed suicide by hara-kiri.

Saigo's head was later recovered by the victorious government forces. The man who conducted the *kubi-jikken* (ceremony of identifying the enemy's head) in the old samurai fashion was General Aritomo Yamagata, who subsequently became Emperor Meiji's elder statesman and lived well into the twentieth century. He had known Saigo well as an erstwhile colleague in Tokyo before disagreement made the man from Satsuma withdraw from the government. As he now looked on the lifeless head before him, Yamagata's heart was saddened, it was said, by the sudden demise of a man whose great talents had been squandered so vainly.

Saigo's bronze statue that today stands on a height

at the southern gate to Ueno Park has the same air of unruffled strength he assumed in life. Were he alive today, he would undoubtedly be a sad man in this age of the remorselessly impersonal machine war. Wars are now won or lost in the laboratories, and the personal qualities of valor and leadership in the field, which he so brilliantly exemplified, are no longer decisive factors. Saigo, in truth, seems today like a figure from a far remote past, for since that time man has made almost inconceivable strides in the acquisition of means of destruction. From Shiroyama to thermonuclear fusion seems an eon in time, but Saigo lived only a little over eighty years ago. There are persons still living who can recall that day when Saigo's head fell and his name became a legend.

8

Asakusa

Girls, Glamor,
and a Golden Goddess

NORTH OF NIHOMBASHI AND NOT FAR FROM Ueno is Asakusa, Tokyo's glorified amusement center.

There has always been an affinity between sex and religion in the pleasure places of Japan. Wherever people congregate for amusement, there you will find temples of religion standing cheek by jowl with palaces of pleasure.

Nowhere is this more apparent than in Asakusa, where the showhouse stars along amusement row perform almost within earshot of the solemn cathedral of Kannon-sama. Here, in the oldest part of the city, people come either to be amused or to find spiritual solace. There are shops of all sorts here, of course, and there are also dining places, some of them of good quality, offering inexpensive fare served in varying degrees of amplitude. Traditionally, the Edokko is something of a gourmand, and he has always cherished a soft spot in his heart for the eateries of Asakusa. But even so, the attraction of Asakusa's restaurants tends to become of secondary importance before the lure of the showhouses, which range from the shabbiest strip places to the palatial Kokusai Theater, where Tokyo's most extravagant revues are produced.

Asakusa earns its biggest income from the amusement places in the Rokku district. The commodities sold here are spectacles, excitement, and glamor. In front of the theaters where spielers blare forth their hyperboles, pleasure seekers gather and disperse and gather again, in eddies and waves. Edokko and out-of-towners here rub shoulders carelessly in the camaraderie of fun, enjoying the mood, the sights, and the sounds.

Here also, along the crowded ways, nude figures of women twenty feet tall look down from signboards in front of revue houses. Other places have other attractions, some purveying musicals, others screen dramas, comedies, or vaudeville.

Then there are the places for samurai dramas, a perennial favorite. Here every night heroines are abducted and villains slain, and brave warriors commit hara-kiri in purple tragedies. In the packed houses, the odor of sweat and the shopgirls' perfumes on a hot summer night may be a little heady for the squeamish, but for the local merchants this is the smell of prosperity. For them, the customers who patronize their shows are what keeps Asakusa's lights aglow and the cashbox jingling.

Side by side with those seeking diversion is another set of visitors with another mission in mind. They are the faithful ones, humble but great of number, who make their solemn pilgrimage to the great temple of Kannon-sama.

For sheer number and variety of people, from the lower middle class to the lowest segments of society, there are few places which offer such a fascinating close-up of the human scene. Asakusa is a cup that flows over with the joys and tears of the little people.

142

At first glance, Asakusa seems to be perpetually on parade. The merry-go-round seems never to stop, with neon signs atwinkle and music flowing from every shop and cafe. But behind the glitter and the tinsel, the seamier aspects of the very poor cast long shadows here, especially after the visitors have departed at night and darkness closes in. It is then that the stall keepers close up shop and show-girls walk home by twos and threes in the almost deserted streets. About this time, too, the homeless ones settle down for the night in some convenient corner.

The crowds here move as regularly as the tides. They begin collecting in strength about noon, reaching full flood just after dark, and ebbing abruptly before midnight, leaving behind only the nightclubs and a few other places of dubious character to keep up the after-midnight carousal.

A postwar innovation in Asakusa's show world is the appearance of *onna kengeki*, sword dramas presented entirely by female casts. Originally performed by mixed casts of males and females, in Asakusa's *kengeki* row girls of fetching physique and assorted talents have begun to take over dual roles, impersonating fabled swordsmen in melodramas of blood and thunder. They wear male costumes, wield swords with amazing agility, and decapitate villains whenever and wherever necessary for the delectation of not-too-discriminating audiences. These dramas are, in a sense, a Japanese counterpart of the Western horse opera, with their themes of honor, love, and violent death. The on-stage movements of these women actresses are often a marvel of dexterity, kimono flying and sturdy legs flashing.

As for the burlesque shows, these bloomed into popularity soon after the end of war. The follies type of show had always been a feature at Asakusa, but the American-style striptease is a postwar phenomenon. It was first introduced at the other end of Tokyo, but soon found itself firmly established at Asakusa where, for a time, six strip places competed for customers simultaneously.

Some of the brightest names of Japanese show business had their start in Asakusa. This was their finest school. Their art was forged in the rough, tough ways of an exuberant crowd that expresses its fiercely partisan likes and dislikes in no uncertain terms—all in the old tradition of Edokko. Such veterans as the opera singers Rikizo Taya and Yoshie Fujiwara, the movie actress Yuko Mochizuki, and the television star Enoken all profess their debt to the training Asakusa gave them.

The entertainment places are Asakusa's lifeblood, but her pride and glory is Kinryuzan Senso-ji (Golden Dragon Temple), more commonly known as the Kannon Temple because it is dedicated to Kannon-sama, the goddess of mercy.

Some distance in front of this cathedral stands Kaminari-mon, or Gate of the Thunder God, which was rebuilt in 1960 in the exact image of the one which was destroyed by bombs in World War II. Beyond the gate is a thoroughfare cannily decorated at all seasons to encourage the spending mood of the customers who throng here. The shops are bright with wares. Whether sightseers or pilgrims, the people flow slowly towards the plaza at the other end. And there, in the center of a gravelled square, stands the temple, soaring upward as a great grey bulk, dwarfing all other buildings around it.

In front of the temple is the Koro, a structure fashioned of bronze, sheltered by a roof, and containing an immense incense burner. Here, on any day, rain or shine, columns of incense rise slowly, and believers, rich or poor, gather to bathe themselves in the mystic fumes.

Ills of man are many and varied, ranging from thinning hair to epilepsy, ague, and blindness. Sufferers of these and other ailments come to the Koro in uncounted numbers seeking relief, and they come with a humility born of suffering. Although medical science in Japan is rated among the foremost in the world, no less noteworthy is this deep-seated piety that exists side by side with science. This faith is as old as man—and universal—whether in Asakusa, beside the Ganges, or in the waters of the Jordan.

Young or old, male or female, the pilgrims all stand by the Koro's open sides, thrusting their hands into the smoke-filled pot and fanning the fumes in their own direction. Each in his own way, they rub the smoke on their bodies in the belief that by so doing they will be rid of the sundry malaises that afflict them in illness or old age.

Here, for instance, an old man with rheumatic joints massages them with the acrid smoke. Nearby, a grandmother with failing sight cups her thin hands to catch a wisp of the sacred smoke in the hopes that it will rejuvenate her eyes. Then there are the tubercular patients, who inhale the smoke briefly, coughing and choking, in the faith that by this act of penance the all-merciful goddess will restore their wasted lungs.

Beyond the Koro are the wide steps leading to the stately abode of Kannon-sama. The temple was rebuilt after the Allied bombings had destroyed its hardy predecessor that had withstood fires and earthquakes for more than three centuries. The interior of the new structure is impressively large, extending 110 feet in each direction under a high ceiling that is supported by massive pillars. As pilgrims pass through the front portal, heavy with lacquered moldings, they are confronted inside by an array of somberly beautiful furnishings, illuminated by flickering candles. Here are altars, images, and incense burners. Priests in gorgeous vestments preside at service time, their deep-voiced intonations rising and falling like music.

As pilgrims look up, their eyes are intrigued by the picture of a dragon painted on the ceiling. It is a large creature, coiling fearsomely and clutching a jewelled orb. Legend says that the serpent, the Japanese symbol of Fate, lived for a thousand years on earth and a thousand years in the sea before soaring to heaven seeking the great jewel.

The jewel is said to represent man's aspirations, and the dragon is therefore a good omen. People born in the year of the dragon, they say, are not only wise and gifted, but are also abounding in energy, like this giant serpent that can scale the heights to heaven in one furious leap from the sea.

This painting of the *ryu*, as the mythical creature is called, is a masterpiece from the brush of Ryushi Kawabata. The painting is a large one, measuring twenty-one feet by seventeen feet. On either side are two angels, both painted by Insho Domoto, who received the nation's cultural medal several years ago for his contribution to art.

In front of the main altar is a huge offertory box where pilgrims stand, heads bowed and rosaries in hand. It lies under a hanging lantern that is as big as a house. Amid the jingle of coins that keep showering into the casket, the faithful clap their hands here and offer their prayers in a manner that has prevailed without change for a thousand years.

The Feast of Lanterns, falling on August 15, is the temple's most important festival. On that day the grounds swarm with believers. Clothed in their fairest finery, both children and grownups gather to take part in the annual festivities of Obon. This is the day on which, according to Buddhist tradition, the spirits of departed relatives and ancestors return to earth for a brief reunion with the beloved kinsfolk they left behind. On this day, in both rural and urban districts, rice wine and the favorite foods of the departed ones are offered at their graves or at family shrines. After the ghostly visitors have been suitably consoled at their homecoming by these symbolic gestures of hospitality, the fun begins. There is feasting at home, and the dancing to Obon music in the neighborhood squares and parks is one of the perennial joys of Japan.

During the Obon festival the grounds of Kannon Temple are crowded and the mood is gay. Sidewalks are all but obliterated by vendors who dispense their wares from rows of stalls. The holiday-makers are not only brightly dressed, but they come immaculately cleansed by long and leisurely immersion in the bathtub. Thus purified, and in a mood of happy expectancy, entire families are prepared to meet their ancestors under the blessings of Kannon-sama.

Finally, after sundown, the all-important moment comes. Amid prayers and the ringing of gongs, all join in the solemn procession to the nearby Sumida River, where priests in robes stand on the riverbank chanting their ancient ritual while large numbers of candle-lit lanterns are set adrift downstream and out to sea. Each candle is a prayer, and each lantern carries with it the hopes of its giver. The lights rise and fall, their reflections dancing in the water, until they finally vanish altogether into the darkness.

Almost as important, and certainly more spectacular in its celebration, is the temple's Dragon Festival, observed twice each year on March 18 and October 18. Legend says a golden dragon appeared from heaven on the day the image of Kannon-sama was enshrined here many ages ago, during the reign of Empress Suiko. The festival is highlighted by the appearance of a man-made dragon of immense size—a fierce-looking monster with a mouth as large as a barrel. Borne aloft on poles by a group of agile young men, the serpent coils about and dances energetically through the streets, to the delight of the crowds that collect here for the spectacle.

The most famous single object of the temple, however, remains an enigma. Over teacups and in halls of learning, a controversy has developed over this mystery which defies solution because the key evidence is withheld from mortal eyes. Some say that the golden image of Kannon-sama that is reputed to be enshrined here does not really exist at all—that it is a legend, albeit an intriguing one. Others swear that its existence is an incontestable verity, as real as the goddess' charity is boundless.

Some years ago a reporter approached a priest of the temple to ascertain the truth regarding the mystic treasure. The priest was a person wise in the ways of men, and he replied, in substance, in this fashion: By profession, a newspaper writer must necessarily deal with tangible things needing tangible proof, but a priest deals with verities of the spirit that transcend physical evidence. He knows Kannon-sama exists because the heart tells him so, just as millions of believers have been moved by this same mystic wisdom of the soul ever since the golden image, reputedly only two inches tall, was hauled up from the nearby Sumida River in a fishing net by the Hinokuma brothers, Hamanari and Takenari, on March 18, 628. The two brothers have since been enshrined in Sansha Shrine, which stands to the side of the Kannon Temple.

The priest then went on to tell the following history of the temple:

The story of the Most Radiant One first became widely known in the Genroku era, but Kannon-sama has reposed behind her inviolate sanctuary for more than thirteen hundred years. After the passage of so many centuries, the reliquary containing the Divine One has decayed and others have been deposited over it in threefold layers, all of them still intact and inviolate within the temple's holy of holies. In times of fires that have repeatedly destroyed the temple, the sacred objects have always been borne to safety without violating their secret.

In the period after the Restoration nearly a hundred years ago, an event occurred which profoundly stirred the hearts of believers. In the confusion of the time, several minor officials of the government appeared on the scene armed with a scroll purporting to be an imperial order. They demanded, under threat of chastisement, to see the sacred image. The priests who were present at this moment of sacrilegious exposure were all holy men, and bowed their heads low in humility, so they did not behold the Kannon-sama as she was slowly taken out of her sanctuary.

On the other hand, the government officials who had come with the singular demand presumably saw the figurine, but they did so not without tribulation. After committing this act of sacrilege they died one by one under mysterious circumstances as yet unexplained, and no mortal eyes have since lighted on the Most Serene Goddess of Charity.

The original temple on this spot was erected in the seventh century by Saint Shokai, father of the faith, who devotedly carried out the divine injunction he received in a dream, which commanded him to preserve Kannon-sama from all mortal gaze.

The particular temple which the shogun Tokugawa Iemitsu built in the seventeenth century in adoration of his patron deity stood on this spot until the closing phase of World War II. It had been a holy place of wide renown. Shogun, holy men, and great figures of history worshiped in its chapel. Then on that fateful day, March 10, 1945, fire produced by Allied bombing destroyed the temple completely within three hours. As in all previous fires, the sacred object was carried away to safety, its secret unviolated.

In the thirteen centuries that went before, the priest concluded, the temple had burned down no less than twenty times, but each time it was rebuilt by Kannon-sama's boundless goodness and through the sacrifices of the faithful. Such was the case again following the war, when the present structure was built.

Visitors, who include tourists, pilgrims, and funseekers, are the indispensable ingredients of Asakusa's prosperity, but no less important—and far more interesting—are the people of Asakusa themselves. They form a tight society, with a pride of their own and a tradition that goes back even before Nihombashi was in existence.

As part of a postwar trend, outside influences have invaded Asakusa in considerable numbers, so that most of the showgirls today and a good proportion of the waitresses are now commuters from elsewhere. But there still remains a hard core of natives who are rooted to their soil. Asakusa is one of the last strongholds of the true Edokko, surviving amidst the rise of the new generation devoted to jazz and sophistication.

Despite the new inroads, old Edo's piquant flavor and quaint ways are still preserved here. One detects them in shop signs, place names, and in old culinary practices. The rituals observed here during festivals are centuries old. At the beginning of the new year, for instance, local maids still walk the streets with their hair done in *marumage*. This elaborate traditional coiffure is adorned with ornaments called *kanzashi*, which are old enough to have been melting girlish hearts since before the golden age of Genroku.

Asakusa has been described as an island of glitter in a sea of poverty. Beyond the amusement center are slum areas where denizens cling to life in squalor and darkness. This poverty all around has always exerted a pressure on Asakusa, where peripheral dwellers inevitably seep in to mingle with the crowds. Assorted characters gather here to eke out a precarious existence. Life for them is cruel, but those who have survived the attrition are a tough tribe, defying extinction. Into the tolerant bosom of Asakusa come seers, mountebanks, fortune tellers, medicine men, evangelists, anarchists, buffoons, and crackpots. There are also quirks of nature, mystics, villains, and bums. They sell every conceivable commodity, from love potions to hypnotism, from bamboo back scratchers to tracts on how to create a utopia in Japan. They harangue skillfully, using all the tricks of the trade. Their pitch is implausibly roseate, it would seem, but there is always a bumpkin willing to rise to the bait.

These traffickers of wit come and go, moving from place to place, always with one eye cocked for the law. Physical crime is rare in Asakusa, and the police box at Kaminari-

mon is among the quietest in Tokyo. To these dubious
characters of curbstone trade, mayhem is anathema, since
it excites attention, bringing policemen on the run. But to
deal in these other "peaceful" professions of wile—that is
another story. To their mind, selling an angel in a glass is
no crime but a service of a sort, since it serves as a lesson to
the gullible. Neither do they see any harm in selling tickets
to a nonexistent peepshow in a nonexistent alley, since such
suckers as would desire to purchase them, in their eyes,
deserve to be taken for a ride.

Not all the people who collect here, however, are drift-
wood from regions below. Some of the greatest names of
history have trodden the streets of Asakusa. Iemitsu the
Magnificent, third shogun of his dynasty, used to worship
here at the Kannon temple. Shogun Ienari was fond of
relaxing here after a hard day at the hunt. Famous actors,
writers, scholars, and tycoons of commerce all have left
behind in Asakusa legends that never fade.

Asakusa also attracted some of Edo's greatest artists. Such
a one was Hokusai. One incident in the fabulous life of this
man, who produced thirty thousand different *ukiyo-e* designs
in his lifetime of nearly ninety years, has become a favorite
part of the Asakusa folklore.

Hokusai was a cantankerous man with a sharp tongue,
but he was also an artist of wondrous capacity. He was full
of whimsy, energy, and bile. His gift of showmanship was
legendary. One day, when he was in his forties, he amazed
all Edo by painting a gigantic portrait of the Indian saint
Daruma in the yard of Gokoku-ji temple. He used a barrel
for inkpot and a broom for brush to create this painting,
which measured some fifty feet across and was so tall that it
had to be hauled up to the eaves of the temple by means of
pulleys.

When the shogun Ienari heard of the feat, he commanded
that Hokusai be brought to Denpo-in temple in Asakusa for
a demonstration of his prowess. Though poor and in rags

most of his life, Hokusai was a proud man, scorning to humble himself even before the mightiest. In the presence of the august shogun and his retinue of courtiers, he betook himself grandly to the center of a vast hall, carrying a mysterious box with him. Unrolling a long sheet of paper, he brushed two parallel lines of blue on its white surface to represent flowing water. Then he opened the box. Out stepped a rooster. He quickly daubed scarlet ink on the bird's feet. As the creature hopped nervously over the paper, it left behind footprints that had the appearance of autumn leaves.

"I have created a landscape for Your Gracious Excellency," Hokusai said, bowing low to the Shogun amid murmurs that rose from the amazed auditors. "It is called *Red Maples Along Tatsuta River*."

9
Tokyo Bay
When Peace Came

TOKYO BAY IS THE FRONT DOORSTEP TO THE
world's largest city. It is a bustling shipping lane and a body
of water whose history goes back to the remotest time. So
vast is the bay that three large rivers (Sumida, Edo, and
Tama) flow into it and three major ports are located along
its extensive shore line.

Aside from its size and commercial importance to Japan,
the bay has been the setting for many historic events both
ancient and modern. Of the ports found here, the Yokosuka
anchorage lies furthest from Tokyo in the outer bay. Here, in
the Meiji era, the old Imperial Navy was founded. Also
based here, in 1905, were the forces which sailed under the
command of Admiral Togo to destroy the Russian fleet in
the straits of Tsushima during the Russo-Japanese War.
And from here, in 1941, Vice Admiral Nagumo's task force
steamed out for the attack on Pearl Harbor.

North of Yokosuka is Yokohama. A relative latecomer as

ports go, Yokohama (then known as Kanagawa) was developed only toward the end of the Edo age. It was here, in 1854, that Commodore Perry concluded a treaty with the Tokugawa regime for opening up Japan to the world. A stern disciplinarian, the proud Yankee commodore was a methodical planner, with a canny sense of history. He was fully aware of the significance of what he was doing, and he did it with dignity and firmness (see Chapter 10).

After forcing the Treaty of Kanagawa upon the reluctant Bakufu, Perry set about exploring the bay. His armor-clad vessels appeared to the local inhabitants like smoke-breathing monsters as they steamed right up to Edo's doorsteps, taking soundings. To the Japanese, who were just then emerging from 250 years of isolation, the spectacle was so thoroughly alarming that they hastily began constructing fortifications of their own to repel any further incursions. Though never actually used in battle, a few of the old gun emplacements built at that time can still be seen off Shinagawa.

All along the bay's far-ranging shore lines are vast industrial complexes, some of them built on lands reclaimed from the bay.

Then there is Tsukiji, site of Tokyo's first foreign settlement, established in 1869. Though the old concession at the mouth of the Sumida River was disbanded more than half a century ago, some of the relics still remain. And nearby, in proud grandeur, towers the magnificent Buddhist cathedral of Hongan-ji. The original temple here was built after the fire of 1657 on land reclaimed from the bay. The present edifice is a modern one. Its two bell towers have historic interest. Inside the one on the right reposes a monstrous battle drum ten feet high which is said to have been brought back from Korea by the soldiers of Toyotomi Hideyoshi following their invasion of the neighboring continent in the sixteenth century. Inside the other tower lies the bell which Ota Dokan is said to have once used in Edo

Castle, which he founded in the fifteenth century. Attached to this bell is an electric gadget that, incongruously, ensures automatic tolling.

Another landmark of Tsukiji is its central wholesale market. Because thousands of tons of food are brought here each day to feed some ten million people, Tsukiji is known as the Food Basket of Tokyo. It is the world's largest food center.

Next to Tsukiji is the site of the old detached palace, Hama Rikyu. Though the palace itself no longer remains, the extensive grounds on which it once stood have been converted into a sanctuary for many varieties of wild life. These include flocks of migrating birds that come here annually to sojourn and multiply along the numerous inlets which face the bay.

It was here, in 1879, that Emperor Meiji entertained General U. S. Grant when the hero of the American Civil War stopped on his way home from a tour around the world. The Emperor, then only twenty-six years old, dispatched a special train to Yokohama to welcome Grant, who had arrived with Mrs. Grant aboard the warship *Richmond*. The general was then a mature statesman, having served two terms as president after he had accepted General Lee's surrender at Appomatox. A blunt-spoken soldier who was reared in the rough backwoods of the American Middle West, Grant showed a fatherly interest in his host, a ruler who was less than half his age. Tradition has it that the old soldier exhorted the young ruler to "take the best of the Western civilization and leave the rest" and cautioned him against the dangers of becoming a pawn of the ambitious Western powers that were then engaged in building empires at the expense of backward nations.

An episode equally historic, but mounted on a vaster scale, took place sixty-six years later in the calm waters of the same Tokyo Bay on whose shore, at Hama Rikyu, General Grant had sojourned briefly as guest of the nation.

This later occasion was the signing of the surrender that ended World War II, signaling Japan's total defeat.

A bespectacled man with hair receding from his large forehead climbed the gangway of the battleship *Missouri*, limping heavily on his cane. After him came an officer in uniform, his chest filled with rows of decorations. The two men, who were followed by nine other compatriots of the defeated nation, had come aboard to sign the articles of surrender.

The first man was Foreign Minister Mamoru Shigemitsu, representing the government. A veteran diplomat whose services extended over many years and in many countries, he walked slowly because of his wooden leg, which he had worn ever since his left leg had been blown off in a bomb outrage fifteen years previously in Shanghai.

The other man was General Yoshijiro Umezu, Chief of Staff of the Army. He represented the supreme military command. Somewhat on the portly side, the general showed a slight paunch. He walked stiffly erect in the manner of his profession.

With the attention of the world focused upon the scene by radio, the deck of the 45,000-ton warship was crowded with men. In addition to the brass and gold braid of men representing the conquering nations, hundreds of war correspondents and cameramen filled all available space on the deck and every other point of vantage.

As Shigemitsu sat at the table to affix his signature, he paused a moment, as if to reflect upon all the vain sacrifices in lost lives and expended miseries his people had endured in their phantom search for an empire. Though no account exists of just what he thought at this historic moment, he was a man of literary taste, and he must have known those classic lines that begin: "In the tolling of the bell of the Gion Temple sounds the transitory nature of all things. . . ."

Only a few years before, in the full flush of a heady victory, Japanese troops had been reaching out, as conquerors, to the ends of East Asia and the Pacific. But in this hour of surrender . . .

After eight years of a dreadful war, during which his nation had suffered five million casualties and untold expenditures in wealth and human misery, peace had at last returned to Japan. The day was September 2, 1945.

⊛

For Japan it was a long journey from the beginning of war's debacle to this scene of surrender in Tokyo Bay. Particularly the anxious period between the Potsdam Declaration of July 26, 1945, calling for surrender, and the final capitulation—this seemed like an age to a nation bleeding from repeated hammering by B-29 bombers. Needless to say, the country was war-weary. It was tired of war, tired of air raids, and tired too of unfulfilled promises and bootless adventures that never ceased.

Although the common people were sick of the fighting and the dying, the hard core of military diehards were not. How a handful of Japanese leaders, through skill and wisdom, had outmaneuvered the fanatics who sought to maintain and prolong the war constitutes one of the most dramatic episodes of history. By their courage and willingness to take risks, including that of their own lives, they saved perhaps a million lives or more.

If there be any illusions that peace was easily achieved in those confused last few days of war, it is only necessary to point out that the final decision to capitulate was won only by a hairbreadth, and even after the die was cast there occurred such a blood bath of opposition as to seem shocking even to a nation inured to acts of violence in moments of crisis.

In all the debate over acceptance of the Potsdam Declaration, no controversy ever arose over the question of the throne. As a matter of fact, there was a practical unanimity of view that the institution of emperor should be preserved, and that this point should be specifically clarified since no mention of it had been made in the Allied proclamation.

Debate did develop, however, over other conditions which the war party demanded as a condition of capitulation. Summarized briefly, they wanted no occupation of the homeland by the Allies. They also insisted upon voluntary withdrawal of Japan's expeditionary forces and voluntary disarmament and demobilization at home by Japan itself. Lastly, they demanded that the Japanese government itself punish its war criminals.

Since these stipulations obviously had no chance of acceptance by the Allies and insistence upon them would nullify all possibility of peace, the civilian leaders, under Foreign Minister Shigenori Togo's leadership, opposed them with all the resources at their command.

It was a tense moment. The discussions were often bitter, the arguments endless. Even as they argued, the Soviet Union on August 8 abruptly declared war on Japan.

In the meantime, most of the high conferees were fully aware that peace was an urgent matter. To cite only the most obvious realities, food had become scarce due to the Allied blockade. Even more demoralizing was the fact that one by one, with ominous regularity, the flourishing cities of Japan were being reduced to shambles.

Underlining this sense of urgency was the brutal fact that, by the final days of the war, 2,500,000 houses in Japan had been destroyed. In addition, more than half a million others had been removed to clear fire breaks. All told, 22 million persons in the urban areas were routed from their homes to shift for themselves as best they could.

In the face of this staggering crisis, sentiment for peace was mounting within the civilian government. In fact, peace feelers had been sent out by the Foreign Office many months previously, even before the Potsdam Declaration. How, then, is the delay in accepting the Allied terms to be explained? The reason for Japan's procrastination in the face of destruction lay in the fact that the fighting services, the army and navy, had a predominent voice in the Supreme War Council, which exercised priority of authority over the civilian Cabinet.

In the struggle that developed in Tokyo over the issue of surrender, the man who emerged as the most forceful personality was Shigenori Togo. With characteristic forthrightness, the Foreign Minister strenuously opposed the stipulations demanded by the fighting services. To accept them, he was convinced, would be tantamount to rejecting the Allied terms.

As a realist, Togo carried out his self-imposed mission with a stout heart in the face of strong opposition. Also, at critical moments, he managed to make salutary contributions by stiffening up Prime Minister Kantaro Suzuki's vacillating position. Obviously an experienced tactician, Togo steered the internal negotiations with fine skill. He managed to employ the right persons, at the right time, to to break the roadblock.

Space does not permit recounting the endless conferences and the calculated pressures employed by both sides to produce a decision. Suffice it to say, the working team of the War Council, on whose decision the fate of the nation rested, was split three to three, and so deadlocked.

On the side for acceptance of the Allied terms were Prime Minister Suzuki, Foreign Minister Togo, and Navy Minister Mitsumasa Yonai. Yonai, incidentally, was a big man, both physically and in the caliber of his character. He was a taciturn admiral who also had previously served as Prime Minister. Always sparing in his words, he bluntly told his Cabinet colleagues that continuation of the war was impossible. He stressed that his conclusion was based on both spiritual and material grounds.

Those opposed to capitulation included Minister of War Korechika Anami, a fanatically dedicated general who simply refused to admit defeat. At a time when nine-tenths of the country's fleet had been destroyed, nine-tenths of its merchant shipping sunk, and its great cities reduced to smoking ruins, Anami even went so far as to declare that the chances for victory were still even. Despite the handwriting on the wall, this view was grimly supported by General Umezu and Admiral Toyota, the two service chiefs.

In all these maneuvers, General Anami stands out as a figure of tragedy. It may be said of all three oppositionists, but particularly of the War Minister, that they were not necessarily blind fanatics. It is true they were still outwardly full of defiance, scornful of their enemy's might. They were not, however, motivated by courage alone. They were actually hostages of the fanatical junior officers under them who demanded a war to the finish, with the implied threat of violence if their wishes were denied. This was no idle gesture in view of the succession of political murders that had occurred all through the 1930's. It was part of the price a nation paid for the insubordination of its unruly elements who attempted to rule by assassination.

Former Foreign Minister Yosuke Matsuoka canvassed the views of Japan's leading authorities and presented a report stating that at that late date Japan would not be able to obtain even a diplomatically negotiated surrender. Eventually Anami seems to have become convinced of the inevitability of this disgrace, and, according to some sources, it was at this time that he decided to commit suicide, an act which he carried out immediately after the decision to surrender was actually made.

Aside from these willful men, backed by the diehards of the fighting services, there were also blunders by well-meaning friends of peace. One example may suffice.

Prime Minister Suzuki was a doughty former admiral who once served as Grand Chamberlain. It was while he was acting in this capacity as the emperor's adviser that he was miraculously saved from death at the hands of young army officers who stormed into his residence during the abortive insurrection of February 26, 1936. After shooting him down with a pistol, the rebels were about to give him the *coup de grace* (severance of the throat arteries with a sword in the samurai manner) when his wife pleaded with them to spare him this final blow since her husband was already mortally wounded. The army hotheads complied, thinking Suzuki was already at death's door. After the assassins left, however, Suzuki was rushed to the hospital, where physicians managed to save his life.

Suzuki's loyalty to the throne, stemming from personal association with the emperor, was well known to his colleagues. Playing on the aged statesman's concern for the emperor's status, which they warned was in danger, the antipeace faction now began putting strong pressures upon him. Plagued by these new doubts, Suzuki in a moment of weakness told reporters that it was the policy of his government to ignore the Potsdam Declaration. The interview was played up by the press with banner headlines, and the news was flashed by radio to the United States.

The answer that came from the other side was swift and appalling. Hiroshima and Nagasaki were wiped out, on August 6 and 9 respectively.

After protracted vacillation, the final decision in Tokyo came with surprising suddenness. Aside from the Russian threat, this was due in large part to the unfathomable peril of atomic destruction that hung over the nation. As a matter of fact, the United States had in possession at the time only the two bombs, and both had already been expended over the two Japanese cities, but the Japanese of course were not aware of this fact.

In this crisis, and as a last resort, Prime Minister Suzuki resorted to what turned out to be a brilliant piece of strategy that paved the way for the decision of Emperor Hirohito as the final arbiter.

The full-dress meeting of the Supreme War Council

that began shortly before midnight on August 9 took place inside the air-raid shelter of the palace. In addition to the regular members previously mentioned, other high officials were present, including Baron Hiranuma, President of the Privy Council.

As the lengthy debate droned away in the Emperor's presence it soon became evident that the session was once again about to be deadlocked. Among members whose voice really counted, the vote was three against three, with Prime Minister Suzuki keeping silent. Anami and the two service chiefs, Toyoda and Umezu, were for continuing hostilities. On the other side, for peace, were Togo, Yonai, and Hiranuma.

Dramatically, at two in the morning, after hours of vain arguments, the Prime Minister rose and said quietly that he proposed to seek imperial guidance and substitute it for the decision of the conference. This was an unprecedented step, but the old admiral took the course because he knew it was the only one left for saving the nation.

And the Emperor, as the supreme authority in the nation, cast his decision for peace.

Thus, in the final analysis, the deadlock was broken and the war was ended because of the decision of the one person who possessed both the resolution and authority to accept peace. That person was the Emperor.

That night was memorable in more ways than one. The ancient pines in the palace grounds were lit by a brilliant moon, and no air raid took place. As the people slept peacefully in the first quiet night to occur in some time, they were unaware that a historic decision was being made at that very moment, one which was to be their salvation.

In the note to the Allied Powers, the Japanese government accepted the Potsdam Declaration "with the understanding that the said declaration does not comprise any demand which prejudices the prerogatives of His Majesty as Sovereign Ruler." The American reply from Secretary of State James Byrnes was delivered through the Swiss government. In his memoirs, Secretary of War Stimson called this reply a "masterful paper" because it avoided any direct acceptance of the Japanese condition, but "accomplished the desired purpose of reassuring the Japanese." Byrnes' note contained this line: "The ultimate form of government shall, in accordance with the Potsdam Declaration, be established by the freely expressed will of the Japanese people."

Even in face of the overwhelming catastrophe that confronted the nation, the service chiefs remained adamant. By this time, the atmosphere in Tokyo was perilously tense. Hotheaded junior officers were secretly engineering resistance, and this was known to Cabinet members. As the ministers met to consider Byrnes' note, they found that this time the count was twelve to three in favor of acceptance. Despite this emphatic show of will, Suzuki still vacillated. He wanted a unanimity of view, which was clearly out of the question.

In the meanwhile, disorder continued. A bomb was thrown into the Foreign Minister's residence. Inflammatory posters appeared in the streets. Even worse, the Prime Minister began wavering to such an extent that former Foreign Minister Shigemitsu, from Nikko, and former Prime Minister Prince Konoye, from Odawara, had to be hastily summoned to Tokyo to assist Marquis Kido's efforts to stiffen Suzuki's backbone.

The end came on August 14 when the Emperor once again ordered acceptance of the Allied terms. He followed this up by preparing a radio address explaining the course of events and the fact of surrender to a stunned nation.

Even as the great decision was made and the note of acceptance was delivered to the Allied powers, further disorders broke out. Although factories were in smoking ruins all about, and production of war materials had become a mere trickle, plainly indicating that further continuation of war was impossible, fatalistic fanatics were still determined to fight on. Near midnight of August 15, just prior to the Emperor's address, a contingent of the imperial garrison secretly marched out. Their aim was to raise an insurrection. They were led by Colonel Hatanaka and his associate Major Koga, who was former Prime Minister Tojo's nephew. The rebels called upon General Mori, commander of the Imperial Guard Division, demanding actions to nullify the Emperor's decision.

General Mori refused pointblank, whereupon he was shot to death on the spot. Colonel Shiraishi, the general's nephew, tried to shield him but was cut down by saber in the attempt. The rebels then forged an order for the Imperial Guards to occupy the palace in an attempt to seize the phonograph recording of the Emperor's message to the nation explaining the fact of capitulation, which was about to be broadcast over the radio network.

General Tanaka, commander of the Eastern Army Group, arrived posthaste on the scene just as the First Regiment of the Guard Division was about to march into the palace with loaded guns and fixed bayonets. He quickly informed Colonel Watanabe, the commander of the regiment, that the order was a forgery. Astounded by the trickery, the colonel forthwith ordered his troops disbanded.

General Tanaka, an old-style *bushi* (soldier) of unlimited loyalty to the emperor, then rushed to the palace, where in the gloomy hush of the night he addressed the troops of another regiment for hours on end, finally persuading the men to disband. Four of the men, however, out of disillusionment for a cause they now realized was lost beyond recall, committed suicide on the spot.

Elsewhere, pro-peace leaders narrowly missed being assassinated. In this category were such men as Ishiwata,

Minister of the Imperial Household, and Marquis Kido, Lord Keeper of the Privy Seal. The prime minister's official residence was besieged with machine-gun fire, and the private homes of both Admiral Suzuki and Baron Hiranuma were set afire; the men, however, escaped injury. In what was obviously a well calculated plot, other troops occupied broadcasting stations because means of communication were considered to be a key factor in any successful coup.

It was about this time that War Minister Anami committed hara-kiri. Earlier, he had sat on the veranda of his house writing a farewell poem. Then at four o'clock in the morning he faced in the direction of the Imperial Palace and drove a dagger into his belly and then into his neck.

Essentially, Anami was an anachronism. Although as War Minister he had to do with guns and tanks and planes, he never fully understood the totality of modern war. He could not see, for instance, that the men in laboratories who unraveled the secrets of the atom, or the totality of a mobilized economy mass-producing war materials, were as significant in winning modern wars as suicide squads mounting *banzai* charges.

The real tragedy, of course, lay in the fact that men like General Anami and the even more anachronous General Hideki Tojo, wartime Prime Minister, with their parochial vision, were able to assume so much power at a time when the situation called for the highest order of statesmanship to save the nation from catastrophe. Between the two men, however, there was a difference. Anami died cleanly in the samurai tradition, whereas Tojo badly botched his attempt at suicide with a pistol, and had to be rushed to a hospital. As most people know, he was later tried, found guilty, and hanged for war crimes. His ashes were scattered over Tokyo Bay.

Then there was General Tanaka, whom we had occasion to mention earlier. He was a moderate. He also took the road of a soldier's death by suicide, but for another reason. He wanted to make amends to the emperor for the armed disturbance which troops under his command had perpetrated in the palace.

There were many other fatalities in this orgy of bloodletting. General Sugiyama, one of the fiercest advocates of Japan's war program, ended his life later, with his wife, in a double suicide. Four hundred troops from nearby Ibaragi revolted, seizing Ueno Hill, while another contingent took over Atago Hill, both in the heart of Tokyo. Those at Atago, realizing the bankruptcy of their cause, blew themselves up with hand grenades, but those at Ueno were induced to disperse peacefully.

There was confusion and chaos for the whole nation. The people were in a daze. All kinds of wild rumors began spreading, causing endless alarms. One in particular intimated that Yankees were coming to commit atrocities. Men fled from the cities to hide their wives and daughters.

A group of fanatics committed mass suicide in the palace plaza protesting the surrender.

In time a semblance of order returned. The voice of the Emperor had a reassuring effect, and the stage was set for the final act of the drama.

With the death of Anami, the Suzuki Cabinet lacked a War Minister. Marquis Kido, in consultation with Baron Hiranuma, recommended that a new cabinet be formed under Prince Higashikuni, the Emperor's uncle-in-law and a general on the active list. It was under his government that another incipient insurrection on August 20 was quelled. This cleared the way for the new Foreign Minister, Shigemitsu, who had succeeded Togo, and General Umezu to make the journey to the *Missouri* for the signing.

Leaving Shigemitsu a moment as he remained seated before the table on the *Missouri's* deck for the signing, let us note more fully the famous lines from *The Tale of the Heike* which we have already quoted briefly. The wisdom of the ancients may have some pertinency to the more recent Japanese adventure in the heady road to glory. The lines run:

In the tolling of the bell of the Gion Temple
sounds the transitory nature of all things.
The pallid color of the flowers
expresses the truth that the prosperous must fall,
that the proud do not endure for long
but must fade away like a spring night's dream.
And like dust before the wind, the mighty too
will inevitably perish from the earth.

With the attention of the world centered upon him, Shigemitsu boldly signed his name to the document of surrender in a masterful hand. This September 2, 1945, was one of the red-letter days, perhaps the most historic one, in the long memory of Tokyo Bay.

PART 2

OTHER STORIED CITIES

10

The Drama of
Yokohama

THE PORT OF YOKOHAMA, GATEWAY TO AN
empire, is part of the huge Tokyo-Yokohama metropolitan
complex containing a population of more than twelve million people. This largest urban community in the world is
concentrated in a dense mass on the broad Kanto Plain,
from a district many miles north of the nation's capital, at
Akabane, to the southern tip of Yokohama and even beyond
to Yokosuka. Within this vast area lie Tokyo (Japan's largest
city), Yokohama (the fifth largest), Kawasaki (the eighth
largest), and numerous smaller satellite cities.

The two dominant geographical features of this area
teeming with people and factories are the vast expanse of
Tokyo Bay, into which half a dozen rivers flow, and the
majestic cone of Mt. Fuji, visible in the distance on any
clear day.

Yokohama is both old and new. Parts of it, including
what was once old Kanagawa, are centuries old. Historic

Kanagawa was a flourishing post town on the old Tokaido highway in the age of shogun, samurai, and Tokugawa generals. The port of Yokohama is a comparative latecomer. It was only a collection of fishing huts sunning beside a lonely marsh until Commodore Perry arrived in 1853. Since the day that the doughty old sea dog forced a treaty upon Japan's reluctant shogunate, Yokohama has had an eventful career, feeling the first impact of foreign influences that changed the course of the country's history.

Neighboring Kanagawa was an important center long before Perry's arrival. In Edo days, the Tokaido highway between Edo and Kyoto passed through Kanagawa. This was a busy, historic road. The great regional daimyo passed through it in long processions consisting of pennant bearers, porters, captains, and guards in full battle dress. The dignitaries rode in palanquins, hidden from the common gaze behind fine-mesh screens.

In addition to the warrior class, the commoners also traveled here, both afoot and on horseback. Merchants and artisans, montebanks and minstrels, priests, pilgrims, and just ordinary people constantly passed back and forth, making use of the fifty-three post stations suitably located along the way. These offered the wayfarers rest, food, and lodging. Such idyllic scenes were often interrupted by violence, for the Tokaido was also prey to highwaymen, who practiced their profession whenever and wherever they could until the law caught up with them. It was a picturesque road, winding in and out among gnarled pines, farms, woodlands, and peaceful villages asleep in the sun.

We have vivid pictures of life along this road from artists who have left us innumerable *ukiyo-e* prints. Hiroshige was one of them. He illustrated, among others, several scenes of Hodogaya and Kanagawa, now both within Yokohama's city limits, and included these in his series called the *Fifty-three Stations of the Tokaido*. In a print familiar to many Westerners, he portrayed Kanagawa as a picturesque coast town atop a cliff overlooking Tokyo Bay. There, with his eye for human comedy, he humorously depicted a couple of women teahouse attendants dragging reluctant customers into their establishment.

A little more than a hundred years ago the district around Yokohama was quiet countryside, with paddy fields and wooded knolls where wild game roamed freely. The area where the neighboring industrial city of Kawasaki now stands, its factory chimneys belching black columns of smoke, was once a peaceful countryside where peasants in straw sandals tended their orchards and cultivated flowers for market.

All over this area, and likewise on Miura Peninsula stretching southward, wild game proliferated in undreamed abundance. Pheasants cracked the air with their piercing calls, and wild geese and ducks abounded in the marshes. Here also roamed wild boar, woodcocks, deer, monkeys, quail, bears, squirrels, snipe. Tokyo Bay swarmed with fish, from lowly sardines and mackerel to the lordly *tai* or sea bream, prize of all fishermen.

Since those days, the wildlife has been driven out by man, whose smokestacks have fouled the air, whose machines have frightened away both beast and fowl, and whose tainted factory waste has all but exterminated the once abundant life in the streams and bays of this area.

Despite the noise and the factories in its outskirts, Yokohama has a charm that annually draws swarms of visitors from all parts of the world. The city has wooded parks, neat buildings, and hills commanding splendid views. Its heart lies in front of the Sakuragi-cho Station, where the street called Honcho-dori, with its glitter and roaring traffic, passes over the Benten Bridge.

To the south of this busy district the main arteries criss-cross and great commercial houses rise up to pierce the sky line. And not far off is the waterfront, with its Central and South piers, where vessels from ports all over the world come and go in never-ending procession.

Honcho-dori was the main street from almost the earliest

days of the city. Its name has even become part of English slang although the word suffered a sea-change in its crossing over the Pacific. In the 1860's and 1870's, when Yokohama was known for its fleshpots, American and British sailors on shore leave, some of them the worse off for rice wine, often lost their way in the maze of the city's crooked streets. Once they found their way to Honcho-dori, however, they regained their bearings and everything was clear or, as the expression has it, *hunky-dory,* a term corrupted from the original Honcho-dori and meaning "all is well."

Townsend Harris, the first U.S. consul in Japan, successfully negotiated the first Japanese-American treaty of commerce and amity in 1859, and the agreement was signed the following year in Washington. This was followed by similar Japanese treaties with other countries. Foreigners were a curiosity in those early days. There was an acute shortage of suitable housing for them around Kanagawa, since Japan had been isolated from the world for two and a half centuries. To meet this deficiency, the British, American, and French ministers set up their homes and working places in temples, which offered them both space and privacy.

Kanagawa was a bustling town, as noted earlier, but Yokohama was a tiny fishing hamlet far removed from the Tokaido. Here the men of Edo, where the tottering shogunate was in its last days, were determined to isolate the foreigners, largely for political reasons. The country was then in the throes of civil disobedience. Bands of self-styled patriots roamed the country threatening to kill all " foreign barbarians" on sight in protest against the shogunate's acquiescence in opening up the country. To avoid international complications, Ii Naosuke, who was then the Tairo (more or less equivalent to prime minister), was determined to concentrate foreigners in a place where they could be protected from sword-happy assassins. Though his government was shaky and badgered by foes, Ii was a resolute man. He began developing Yokohama, even as he parried

174

off foreign protests against this sudden shift of port from Kanagawa to Yokohama.

To foreign emissaries, Yokohama, which was then a neck of land cut off from the mainland by a marsh, reminded them of Deshima in Nagasaki, where the Dutch traders had been bottled up for nearly two and a half centuries. With this unpleasant precedent in mind, the Western ministers tenaciously held out for a port at Kanagawa. Ii and his men kept on building warehouses, homes, and shops for the "foreign guests" in Yokohama, cannily guessing that such abundance of facilities there, at a time when the housing shortage was acute in Kanagawa, would eventually force the foreigners to accept Yokohama. And this was exactly what happened.

In addition to the housing, Yokohama offered other substantial advantages, including deep water ideal for port facilities. The place was bounded in front by the bay and on two sides by canals, and its only land approach in those days was cut off by a swamp spanned by three bridges that were easy to defend against foreigner-hating *ronin* (unemployed samurai).

Yokohama's patron statesman, of course, was Ii Naosuke, the strong-minded official who pushed through the signing of the first Japanese-American treaty. On a conspicuous site in Kamon-yama Park, on an elevation overlooking the entire city, there stands today an imposing statue of him. He appears resplendent in his official robe and headgear. The bronze image reflects something of the powerful will with which this dedicated man carried out his purpose in the conviction that his country must either open up its gates and join the world tide of civilization or perish.

Despite his dedication and statesmanship, Ii Naosuke in life was harassed ceaselessly by assorted fanatics. Antiforeign ruffians roamed the streets, killing foreigners, embarrassing his government. He clamped down vigorously, but the effect of this was only to stimulate more violent opposition to his policies. A group of plotters, mostly samurai from the Mito and Kagoshima clans, plotted to kill him and burn down the foreign warehouses and facilities in Yokohama.

On the morning of the Girls' Festival, March 3, 1860, there was an unseasonable snowfall, and the whole city of Edo was enveloped in mantle of white as eighteen determined men, pretending to be sightseers, loitered near the Sakurada Gate of what is now the emperor's palace. As Ii passed by in a palanquin heavily guarded by swordsmen, assassins from Mito rushed out and stabbed him through the wall of the sedan chair. Arimura Jizaemon then pulled the wounded man out and decapitated him, a martyr to his belief that Japan could achieve greatness only by ending its unnatural seclusion. All the assassins but two were captured or slain, either on the spot or later. The two who escaped lived into the Meiji era.

The real drama of Yokohama, however, concerns an American who, by a strange anomaly of history, won friends for his country at the point of a cannon nearly a decade previously. He was a naval commander who changed the course of history without firing a shot. He did it by diplomacy, backed by a willingness to use force if necessary. He did it with dignity and fairness.

Commodore Matthew Perry was a remarkable man. An executive of ability with enormous capacity for work, he had a passion for detail. He had read all the books on Japan that were available. On his historic voyages to Japan he brought along a Dutch interpreter, thinking, rightly, that the Japanese would be familiar with the Dutch language from their long association with Dutchmen at Nagasaki. Sometimes called "Old Matt" by his men, other times "Old Bruin," he was almost sixty years old when he steamed into what is now Tokyo Bay.

In the tradition of naval men in those days, Perry was

▲ 49

◄ 50

49. The harbor seen from Yamashita Park.

50. Sea travelers who berth in this port do not immediately encounter the storybook Japan.

Yokohama . . .

51. A century ago Yokohama was a small fishing village and Commodore Matthew Perry's paddle-wheel vessels were the first mechanized ships ever to appear in these waters. Now it is a harbor for vessels from around the world.

Kamakura...

52. The beach opposite Enoshima Island.

53. Fishermen launch a high-prowed boat from the shore by Kamakura.

▲ 52

▼ 53

▲ 54

▼ 55

▲ 56

54. The Maidono, where in the twelfth century Lady Shizuka performed her famous dance of defiance before the dictator Yoritomo.

55. Rear of Hachiman Shrine, rebuilt by Yoritomo in homage to his patron god.

56–57. Daibutsu, the Great Buddha, built in the thirteenth century.

▲ 58

58. Heian Shrine, erected in 1895 to commemorate the 1,100th anniversary of the founding of Kyoto.

59. Kinkaku-ji, the Golden Pavilion. Burned to the ground in 1950 by a deranged monk, the present structure was erected in exact copy of the original in 1955.

Kyoto . . .

▲ 59

▲ 60

▼ 61

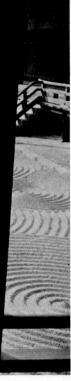

60. The lovely rock and sand garden of Tofuku-ji, one of the city's estimated 1,600 Buddhist temples.

61. A contemporary master of the tea ceremony, engaged in the ritualistic preparation of the tea.

62. Likeness of Sen no Rikyu, greatest of the tea masters, who ended his life by hara-kiri at the command of Hideyoshi.

▲ 63

63. Shisen-do, a temple which preserves the ancient tradition of being a sanctuary for quiet meditation.

64. One of the several buildings of Katsura Detached Palace, regarded as one of the finest examples of both architecture and landscape gardening in Japan.

65. A section of the rock garden of Ryoan-ji; there are fifteen stones in all, arranged in five separate groups.

▲ 64

▼ 65

66. Gion Matsuri, Kyoto's most famous festival, takes place from July 16 to 24 and includes four days during which floats such as this pass through the city's streets. The festival dates back to the year 876.

proud, portly, and blunt of speech. Japanese artists of the time made many portraits of him, and they all depict him as a formidable man with a stern face, an abundance of locks that curled around his neck, and heavy black eyebrows. A canny Yankee bargainer, he knew how to use just the right amount of pressure, in his somewhat pompous way, to get what he wanted—even if he had to bare his guns and menacingly sail his men-of-war around Tokyo Bay to get the results he sought.

Japanese artists, with acid in their brush and imagination in their souls, created a whole galley of pictures that dealt with the coming of Perry. Through these pictures and contemporary accounts, both Japanese and American, we can today easily visualize how the commodore looked, how he and his men comported themselves in ceremonious fashion of his liking, and how his "black ships of evil mien" startled the Japanese when these vessels sailed, breathing black smoke and churning the water with revolving fins (paddle wheels) from Uraga to the south up to the very approaches of Edo.

Perry's mission was greatly assisted by the fast deteriorating situation within Japan itself. However strictly the Bakufu tried to enforce a tight bockade against foreign intercourse, the task became manifestly impossible as the first half of the last century rolled on. The wall began crumbling as the nation's bright young men, full of energy and curiosity, began peering outside, trying to learn how the other world lived and progressed while their own country slept.

A trickle of Western knowledge flowing through the tiny Dutch settlement in Nagasaki only whetted their appetite. The bolder ones, sometimes by chance and other times by connivance, slipped out to foreign countries, at the risk of dire punishment when they returned. Joseph Heco (Hamada Hikozo), Nakahama Manjiro, and Niijima Jo were the most conspicuous of these daring travelers who came back with wondrous tales of foreign progress, further undermining support for the anachronistic, feudal order of society at home.

Other men remained at home but pursued Western knowledge surreptitiously. Such pioneers of thought as Sugita Gempaku, Maeno Ryotaku, and Takano Choei braved persecution, surmounting incredible difficulties, to master Western science and learning. These rebels of the mind found support from other sympathizers, and together they shook the wall of isolation, by then more like a sieve than a barrier. The wall was approaching collapse about the time Perry arrived.

While it is true that the country in any case would have been opened up eventually, Perry hastened the process, and historians now agree his coming was a blessing in disguise at a time when a weak Japan, left to the mercy of less scrupulous men than Perry, could have suffered the fate of other victims of nineteenth-century colonialism.

There was in Perry something of the practical rectitude of the New England preacher with a Bible in one hand and a musket in the other. The letter which he delivered for President Fillmore saluted the emperor as "Great and Good Friend" and contained these words:

"I have no other object in sending him [Commodore Perry] to Japan but to propose . . . that the United States and Japan should live in friendship and have commercial intercourse with each other.

"The Constitution and laws of the United States forbid all interference with the religious or political concerns of other nations. I have particularly charged Commodore Perry to abstain from any act which could possibly disturb the tranquility of your imperial majesty's dominions."

In his kindliest terms the American president summed up the case in his letter by requesting "friendship, commerce, a supply of coal and provisions, and protection for our shipwrecked people."

It was no easy task, however, to deliver the President's letter, and it took all of the old commodore's resources to accomplish it peacefully. Perry's squadron of four ships—three powered by steam—was headed by the flagship *Susquehanna*. As they hove into view in July, 1853, off Uraga some miles south of present Yokohama, consternation spread all the way to Edo. All through the first night, according to accounts still preserved, Perry's men saw beacon fires burning on hillsides and heard great bells tolling as the people pondered the meaning of this strange invasion.

When a functionary of Uraga came aboard the next day in silken robes embroidered with a pattern of peacock feathers, Perry's men, by a combination of tact and firmness, convinced him that the American president's letter should be delivered to a representative of the emperor, and to no one else. Perry, in particular, rejected all thought of sailing to Nagasaki, where the shogun's men wanted him to go. The negotiations lasted six days before an agreement was reached for the Americans to land at the beach of Kurihama near Yokohama.

With the fastidiousness of a man aware that he was about to make history, Perry spent a long time preening himself before the mirror, smoothing out his unruly curls and buttoning up his stiff full-dress uniform. Thus dressed in braids and splendor he strode ashore leading some three hundred men who landed from fifteen launches.

Although he was unaware that the man with whom he parleyed was only a minor functionary, since all the shogun's ministers disdained to treat with "foreign barbarians," Perry acted with a majestic dignity which he deemed necessary in order to impress the "emperor's representative" with the importance of his mission. Not for nothing was he called Old Spit and Polish by his men. He knew well the psychological value of flourish in dealing with proud men like the Japanese, and he behaved with decorum and punctilio. As the two men exchanged polite words, Perry

191

delivered the president's letter contained in a box made of rosewood and embellished with gold, the whole having cost a thousand dollars.

Contemporary American artists, particularly Heine, generally pictured their compatriots as smartly disciplined men in uniform while representing the Japanese shabbily dressed in ungainly robes. But there was never any question by both American and Japanese artists on the score of Perry's demeanor, which was dignity itself.

After he delivered the letter, in a show of force Perry sailed up the bay to within sight of Edo's suburbs in defiance of the Bakufu's edict and then left Japan with the announcement that he would return in the following spring for the emperor's reply. This he did, in February of the following year (1854), when he was accompanied by two thousand men in a squadron of nine ships. This time Perry brought along many gifts, partly to soften the "emperor's men" with a show of generosity, partly to impress them with the mechanical wonders of his country.

For a people unaccustomed to modern inventions, the gadgets which the Japanese received proved fascinating gifts. These included a telegraph instrument with one mile of wire, a telescope, firearms, clocks, and a hundred gallons of whisky. This last item must have tasted potent indeed to a people who were in the habit of taking liquor no stronger than rice wine. To add a note of scholarship to his munificence, Perry bestowed a four volume set of Audubon's *Birds of America*, *Quadrupeds* by the same author, and a Noah Webster dictionary.

Much has been written of the simple-minded antics of the native people who bustled about in wonderment around these ingenious gifts, but what is often missed is that the Japanese were at the same time profoundly shocked by their own inadequacy in the face of the Western proficiency these toys represented. Thus they were convinced that they too must somehow master this technology, if for no other reason than their own survival. The history of Japan's subsequent decades was one of a headlong race against time for wholesale modernization, transforming this once fantastically outdated land to a world power within half a century.

On a cold wintry day, Perry's gifts were carried onto a beach near Yokohama. Few historians can resist retelling the story of what followed: of bewildered Japanese puzzling over the telegraph instrument, wondering how the message got through so swiftly, and rushing from the sending to the receiving end in a vain attempt to beat electricity. Then there was a miniature locomotive, which puffed its way round a circular track with amazed but happy joy riders clinging frantically to the Lilliputian cars, their swords clanking against their sides and their samurai robes flying in the air. After the fun was over and the top-knotted dignitaries were ready for the more solemn duty before them, both sides got down to affixing signatures on the first treaty between the two countries. This took place in what was then the little fishing village of Yokohama. Known as the Treaty of Kanagawa, the agreement opened the ports of Hakodate and Shimoda to American ships for supplies and trade. It also provided protection for shipwrecked mariners, and an American consul was to be allowed to live in Shimoda. It was signed on March 31, 1854.

After the Japanese had entertained the visitors with *sumo* wrestling, the Americans reciprocated, in a grand manner, with a lavish feast aboard the *Powhatan*. The commodore and his captains and the high commissioners of Japan dined below deck. Outside, on the main deck, Perry's subordinate officers feasted with the lesser Japanese functionaries on long tables loaded with fine foods. There were all kinds of zesty fare, including lamb, beef, poultry, fish, fruits, and vegetables, all this topped with champagne and maraschino. Before the dinner was over, the party was uproarious, with friendly spirit prevailing all around.

For entertainment, the Yankee host provided the Japanese with an old-fashioned minstrel show. There, Sambo and Bones, in blackface, went through their side-splitting routine, which even the guests enjoyed despite the barrier of language. The whisky and champagne warmed their hearts, made some of them stagger slightly. One of the Japanese functionaries, a bit gay from the imbibing, threw his 'arm around Perry's neck in a spirit of camaraderie, crushing Old Matt's gold epaulets. Mumbling something about the hearts of Japan and America being one and united, this early harbinger of international good will then toddled off the boat, while a salute of seventeen guns boomed from the *Saratoga*.

In the little more than a century of time that has elapsed since that day, much has happened in this great port. In the first flush of early anti-foreignism, foreigners were as-saulted. Emperor Meiji, in a historic procession, passed through the town on his way to Tokyo from Kyoto in 1868 to assume the reins of monarchy. Amid national rejoicing, the first railway connecting Yokohama with Tokyo was opened in 1872. General Grant stopped here on his way to visit the emperor seven years later. The city was devastated by the great earthquake and fire of 1923; it was leveled once again by the incendiary bombs of the last war.

All these stirring events, both good and evil, have helped to shape Yokohama, but adversity has never crushed the spirit of its citizens. On the contrary, they have rebuilt their beloved city, each time on a larger and more beautiful scale, until today it stands as one of the world's most interest-ing ports. Behind its stately facade, however, there is always the great tradition of Ii Naosuke Kamon no Kami, who opened up Japan, and the timeless episode of the great American sea lord who gave Japan to the world and the world to Japan without firing a shot.

11

Kamakura

Cradle of Valor and Intrigue

ENTERING A CAVERN IN A HILL BEHIND THE Great Buddha of Kamakura, we were confronted by the figure of the goddess Benten, wrapped in the coils of a serpent. This Japanese deity, who serves as guardian of the arts, stood in a niche. Below her was a spring where water seemingly welled out of solid rock. There, a young lady was absorbed in an unusual task. In one hand she held a bamboo basket containing paper money of ¥500 and ¥1000 denominations. With the other she was swishing the notes energetically in the shrine's sacred water.

The goddess in whose honor this shrine is dedicated is called the Zeni-Arai (money-washing) Benten. Legend says that money rinsed here multiplies a hundred or a thousand fold. Countless people each year, from bar madams and geisha to industrial tycoons, troop here in unending flow, all eager to increase the riches they have acquired in Japan's current prosperity. As they come here in their holiday finery, their purses bulging with money, the happy pilgrims seem never to be troubled by any doubt about the efficacy of the ritual. Occasionally a more ingenious pilgrim, in search of quick wealth, can be spotted with a jug or two in which to carry home the magic water so that he can wash his money at leisure whenever he needs new riches.

This custom is only one of the many fascinating facets of the jewel that is Kamakura, Japan's ancient center of government, which today lies dozing in the sun only an hour away from Tokyo by train.

Kamakura is rich in legend and history, and dominated by the colossal figure of Buddha. No matter how often one has seen photographs of the bronze statue, the first actual vision of this masterwork is one of complete astonishment. Lafcadio Hearn long ago described the experience in these words: "The gentleness, the dreamy passion-lessness of those features—the immense repose of the whole figure—are full of beauty and charm. You look up into the solemnly beautiful face—into the half-closed eyes that seem to watch you through their eyelids of bronze as gently as those of a child, and you feel that the image typifies all that is tender and calm in the Soul of the East."

Yoritomo, the twelfth-century ruler who laid the basis of Kamakura's ancient glory, had an indirect hand in the erecting of the sacred statue. Legend says that he and his consort Masako, after inspecting the older and bigger Buddha in Nara in 1195, returned home determined to build a similar statue in their own Kamakura. Yoritomo died before he could realize his dream, but the project was brought to fruition shortly afterwards by the efforts of a determined priest, Joko, with the assistance of Inada no Tsubone, a lady in Yoritomo's court. Riding the crest of a religious revival, they collected funds from believers all over the land and built a huge wooden image, with a temple to house it. The work was completed in 1243, but before a decade had passed, a storm destroyed both the image and the temple. Casting of the present bronze figure was undertaken by Goroemon, who completed it in 1252.

The placid lines of the Great Buddha show Grecian influences that had come to Japan by way of India and China. It is a superb statue, regarded by many as a work of art incomparably superior to the Great Buddha in Nara. As one stands at Hase by the sea in Kamakura and gazes up at the statue's massive countenance, one is struck by the timelessness of its repose. The Buddha has sat there, rain or shine, through peace and war, for seven long centuries, and will doubtless continue to do so for another millenium. Epochs and eras have passed by without ruffling its eternal calm under the stars and the sun, unperturbed by irreverent modern lovers who dedicate love poems to the statue, addressing it variously as Handsome Fellow, Lonely Man, or Poor Saint Who Knows Not Love's Tender Passion.

The Great Buddha, towering forty-three feet in the air, is too impressive a figure to be disturbed by such petty impudence. Its face alone is eight feet high. Its gentle, dovelike eyes are fashioned of pure gold and measure nearly four feet across. The long-enduring relic has remained unsheltered since the year 1495, when a tidal wave rolled up the little valley and smashed the temple housing it.

The Great Buddha, however famous, is by no means the only attraction of Kamakura. Though its population is swollen today to some 100,000 people, the city still remains the peaceful resort for sun seekers that it has been for generations. Because of its mild climate, Kamakura is a favorite refuge for artists, writers, and stage celebrities. Here also congregate followers of the arts of flower arrangement and tea ceremony, while devotees of *zazen* (Zen meditation) practice their cult in the city's many monasteries.

Although this ancient citadel is permeated with antiquity, not all is serenity in its temple-studded walks. In summer, hordes of holiday makers take over the city. They swarm along the beaches, cluttering up every inch of space clear up to Enoshima Isle and beyond in the north and down to Hayama in the south.

Near the latter town, at Zushi, stands a stone memorial marking the spot where the heroine of the novel *Hototogisu* is said to have walked with her husband on their honeymoon. Her name was Namiko. Now all but forgotten, nearly half a century ago Namiko was the symbol of the faithful wife. Roka Tokutomi, who wrote the lachrymose novel, based his story partly on contemporary figures. Namiko's father has been identified as Field Marshal Oyama, who led the Japanese forces to victory in the battle of Mukden in the Russo-Japanese War of 1904-5.

The pallid bride suffered many woes. She was a consumptive and became the victim of a ruthless mother-in-law. This lady of tears became the heroine of a whole generation of readers—a moving figure in the protest against the archaic family system that sacrificed personal integrity to the family code. In the romantic tradition of Meiji literature, Namiko died heartbroken, after having been forcibly separated from her husband. Zushi's town fathers may have had one eye on the tourist trade when they erected the monument in Namiko's memory, but it also serves another purpose. To some people it is a reminder that, despite all the strides that have been made in the emancipation of Japanese womanhood since Namiko's time, Japan's old family system still sometimes intrudes to hound newly-weds.

To the north of Kamakura is Enoshima, a fairy isle on a fairy sea, and behind the island Mt. Fuji soars like a lovely vision. The once-wooden Benten Bridge, extending low and long across the watery flat between island and mainland, is now made of concrete. On the mainland side is Marine-land, where baby whales and adult porpoises cavort and play. The sun-drenched beaches here sometimes attract half a million visitors a day. They are lined with amusement places, villas, and hotels, which have caused the area to be called the Miami of Japan, although it is a noisier, gaudier, and more congested playland than its American namesake. Enoshima likewise provided the setting for a famous novel, Thomas Raucat's *Honorable Picnic,* one of the most sympathetically and penetratingly humorous novels ever written about Japan as seen through the eyes of a Westerner.

Despite the shrill invasion of summertime, Kamakura on the whole is a charming town. It is loveliest in spring, when azaleas and flowering plum and cherry blossoms scent its every hill. Emerging from Kamakura Station, one sees Mt. Fuji on the left, while to the right stands Hachiman, the impressive shrine of the war god. Sauntering up the slope toward Mt. Daijin, past a huge *torii* (shrine gate) and a small lacquered bridge, one is magically transported in time and setting to the feudal splendor of twelfth-century Kamakura.

Amid this lovely setting of an ancient culture, citizens to this day observe picturesque customs that have been handed down through the ages. April 3, for instance, is the beginning of the long spring festival that starts at Wakamiya Shrine, situated below and to the right of Hachiman. April 13 is the anniversary of the death of Yoritomo, and the holiday is concluded then with festivities at Shirahata-gu shrine, near Wakamiya. Pink and white cherry blossoms bloom in vast clouds around the shrine, reaching their peak of beauty at almost exactly the time of this pageant each year.

❀

Kamakura is the birthplace of Japanese feudalism. The city was founded by Yoritomo in the latter half of the twelfth century. A natural fortress, it is less than two and a half square miles in area and surrounded on three sides by wooded mountain barriers and on the fourth side by the sea.

What kind of a man was Yoritomo, the soldier-statesman who picked this well-nigh impregnable stronghold as his base for a particular kind of military government that produced a Spartan civilization?

Yoritomo was one of the handful of Japanese military dictators who left indelible imprints on history. The son of a local chieftain, he was orphaned at the age of twelve when his father was killed in battle. He himself was captured and exiled for twenty years on the Izu Peninsula. When he was thirty-two, he raised an army and challenged the Taira, his family's mortal enemy. Defeated in battle, he barely escaped with his life to the stronghold of his family on the Boso Peninsula north of what is now Tokyo.

There, and in the whole of the Kanto area, Yoritomo ably maneuvered his forces, consolidating loyalties among clan chieftains. Finally he settled down in Kamakura, where, to celebrate his success and to give thanks to his patron god, he rebuilt the Hachiman Shrine. As his power grew, he became impatient to test his mettle once more against the Taira, the dominant family that ruled the land from the capital city of Kyoto. By now the Taira had grown soft from living off the fat of the land. Old Kiyomori, their leader, levied excessive taxes, which caused mounting discontent among the people whose support he needed to keep himself in power. He also exercised the privilege of supplying the emperor with a consort from his own family, and this enabled him to rule the country both by imperial blood-ties and his own military power.

All this Yorimoto noted carefully, and he judged the time was ripe to overthrow the Taira. His next feat brought him renown. One night in November, 1180, he ordered an attack upon the enemy across a marsh near Mt. Fuji. The movements of his troops caused a flock of startled water fowl to take to the air with a noisy flapping of wings. Thinking that vast forces were on the move against them, the Taira retreated in panic. Taking advantage of the confusion, Yoritomo won the important victory of the battle of Fuji River.

A little later, as he was about to return to Kamakura, an event took place which had an important bearing on subsequent history. A young man of noble bearing in full battle armor asked to see him at his field tent. The stranger was none other than Yoritomo's younger half brother, Yoshitsune, the most romantic hero in Japanese history.

When their father died in battle, Yoshitsune was an infant. The Taira spared the child's life, much to their later sorrow, on condition that he be committed to the priesthood. The boy grew up with other ideas, however, and at the age of fifteen became a *bushi* in the north country of Oshu, where his family clan had numerous sympathizers. When he heard that his elder brother was raising an army to fight their common enemy, he hastily marched southward to join him. For the first time, the two brothers met at this encampment on the Kiso River amid great rejoicing, and there they exchanged fraternal vows to wipe out their hated enemy.

From this point on, the story of the two brothers was one of glory and tragedy for Yoshitsune, and power and perfidy for Yoritomo. Yoshitsune, a peerless tactician, led his army to victory after victory against the Taira in the west, while his brother, a crafty man, remained behind in Kamakura building up forces for other eventualities he had in mind. In a brilliant operation Yoshitsune routed his enemy in the battle of Ichi-no-tani (see Chapter 15). This victory won for him the title of High Chief Magistrate, an honor conferred upon him by Goshirakawa, the retired emperor. Later he overpowered the Taira at Yashima on Shikoku Island and finally wiped them out forever in the great naval battle of Dan-no-ura near Shimonoseki.

Back in Kamakura, Yoritomo noted all these exploits with misgivings. As this Japanese Achilles sulked in his tent, his heart rankled with jealousy. He ordered Yoshitsune back to Kamakura, together with his captives. When the younger brother complied, the older brother refused to permit him to enter the citadel on the grounds that Yoshitsune had indulged in acts of insubordination. Yoritomo based this quibbling accusation upon the fact that Yoshitsune had accepted a title from the throne without his permission.

At Koshigoe Pass outside Kamakura, Yoshitsune was kept fruitlessly waiting. Finally, in desperation, he sent a pathetic note pleading with his brother for reconciliation on the grounds of family ties. Yoritomo, a congenitally suspicious man, remained adamant. With a heavy heart Yoshitsune pulled his forces along the Tokaido highway clear back to Omi, where he received an imperial mandate from Goshirakawa to chastise his brother.

In lonely hours, Yoshitsune wrestled with himself over his next course. He vacillated between the sentiment of brotherly ties and the instinct for survival. As a military man he must have been fully aware that a quick decision and a lightning attack were an essential ingredient of success, but he was either unwilling or unable to take the plunge. When finally he faced up to the inevitable, his opportunity had already slipped through his fingers, and henceforth his star waned rapidly. On his way to Kyushu to build up a base of operation, his ships were scattered by a storm. He hastily returned to Yoshino in central Japan. There, in an episode famous in Kabuki drama, he sent back to Kyoto his beloved Lady Shizuka, the mistress who had shared all the trials of his battles during his famous Odyssey. Then he went into hiding.

In the meantime, Yoritomo was not standing idly by. A man of great resourcefulness in time of peril, he enlisted the services of the shrewdest court nobles he could muster as his advisers. In a master move to thwart his brother's comeback, he instituted a system of land tenure that was to become, in its broad outline, the basis of the feudal system that lasted for nearly eight centuries, clear down to 1868. In essence, Yoritomo offered military protection to the regional barons in exchange for unquestioning fealty. In an age of wars and mounting insecurity, the scheme worked like a magic. By it Yoritomo was able to knit the nation's whole social fabric into one of pyramiding loyalties that reached down into every corner of the realm. To prevent disaffections, he devised an elaborate system of espionage. With such ingenious instruments to serve him, he remorselessly pursued his brother.

Yoshitsune, for his part, was forced to flee from one place to another like a hounded fox. His position finally became untenable, so he retreated northward back to the refuge of his old patron Hidehira. Now an old man, clan chief Hidehira of the province of Oshu died of illness shortly afterwards. Unfortunately for Yoshitsune, Yasuhira, the man who succeeded Hidehara, was a weakling of devious mentality. He was motivated less by malice than by fright and befuddlement in the face of Yoritomo's terrible fury.

In order to propitiate the tyrant, Yasuhira perfidiously ordered the murder of Yoshitsune, a guest in his own province. The hero of Ichi-no-tani was in his thirty-first year when the end came. His severed head was pickled in sakè and borne to Kamakura in a black lacquer cask.

As might be expected, Yoritomo refused to see the grisly remains. Many of the soldiers he sent to identify the head, however, had been Yoshitsune's comrades-in-arms. They had fought battles with him in the war against the Taira, and now they all wept tears, it was said, as they recalled how valiantly their former young general had led them to victory while his brother stayed safely in Kamakura.

As for Yasuhira, who was responsible for Yoshitsune's

murder, that craven coward met with condign punishment only shortly afterwards. Although he had ordered Yoshitsune's slaying as a propitiatory gesture, this act in itself was not enough to satisfy Yoritomo's greed. Yoritomo sought not merely to eliminate his brother, but he wanted Yasuhira's domain for himself as well. On the pretext that the young sycophant of the north had been too slow in moving again Yoshitsune, Yoritomo dispatched an army against him. Confronted by this new danger, Yasuhira panicked and fled, only to be killed by his own men, who had turned against him.

With the death of Yasuhira, Yoritomo became the undisputed conqueror of all Japan, and in 1192 he acquired the ultimate in power and prestige when he was given by the emperor the impressive title of Seii-taishogun (Barbarian-Subduing Generalissimo).

Yoritomo had a complex character. His shortcomings were counterbalanced somewhat by qualities that place him among the strong rulers of medieval Japan. In appearance he was slightly deformed, his head being large in proportion to his body. An old painting purporting to be his portrait shows him as a man of stately dignity attired in regal robes, but the picture is an idealization. Records show that his demeanor was calm and suave. He was shrewd and crafty, but loyal and magnanimous enough among the men he liked to ensure their abiding loyalty.

On the other hand, he was also a cruel tyrant who trusted no one and put to death even members of his own family without compunction. In his own fashion, he was a religious man. In battle he always carried a small figure of Kannon, goddess of mercy, tucked inside his helmet, and a rosary was always around his wrist. As he built many beautiful temples, enlisting the services of the finest artists and architects of his age, he was thus a great patron of the arts.

His undoubted contribution, among others, was that he breathed new life and vigor into an age whose ruling class had become soft under the leadership of the luxury-loving Taira. Against this, however, is the fact that his was a Machiavellian age of cunning, intrigue, and bad faith, for which he set an unenviable example.

Toward the close of his life, an event further blackened his name. Noriyori was another young brother who, together with Yoshitsune, did yeoman service in the war against the Taira. In fact, Noriyori and Yoshitsune fought most of Yoritomo's battles for him. Despite their contributions, Yoritomo regarded them meanly, even hostilely. The dark malevolence inside him gave him no rest. We have already seen what happened to Yoshitsune.

As for Noriyori, Yoritomo suspected quite groundlessly that this other brother too was plotting to supplant him. In his characteristically ruthless manner he drove Noriyori off to Shusenji in Izu, and there slew him. As for the dictator himself, the end came prosaically enough—and quite soon. He died as the result of a fall from a horse on his way home from a religious ceremony celebrating the completion of a bridge. That was in 1199. He was only fifty-two years old.

When we turn to Yoshitsune, the task of appraising him precisely becomes a complicated matter, for he has been so much the darling of poets and scribes for centuries that a thousand legends have sprung up, making it difficult in many instances for scholars to separate the truth from the fiction. Yoshitsune was a veritable Roland, Hamlet, and Coeur de Lion all rolled into one.

Although he was an unorthodox general of great daring, some of the more fabulous exploits attributed to him are obviously exaggerated. Most authorities now believe, for instance, that the episode in the Kabuki drama *Kanjincho,* depicting him and Benkei as they cross the Ataka barrier in their flight north disguised as itinerant monks, is actually more poetry than truth.

Nothing in Yoshitsune's military career, however, equals

in interest his relation with Lady Shizuka. For her story, we must go back to that point in his career when he reluctantly, and with forebodings, sent her back to Kyoto when his own position in the field became precarious.

Professionally, Shizuka was a *shirobyoshi*, a dancer. In addition to possessing rare beauty sparked by a proud spirit, she exhibited great elan and grace as a dancer. According to ancient accounts, she was a paragon of virtue, sharing all of her man's hardships in battle, sleeping by the roadside with a rock for pillow and the stars to comfort her when the occasion demanded it. Soon after her tearful parting with Yoshitsune in the Yoshino forest, she was seized by Yoritomo's agents and taken to Kamakura. There, by her dramatic behavior, she became immortalized in poetry.

As one goes up the double avenue in Kamakura that leads to Hachiman Shrine from Kamakura Station, one comes upon an open edifice known as the Maidono (Pavilion of the Dance). It is located in sylvan surroundings near a pond with a red bridge spanning it. This is where Lady Shizuka gave her last and greatest performance.

At first she proudly rejected the order to dance before a brilliant assembly consisting of Yoritomo, his consort Masako, and other celebrities. Then she reversed her decision. Instead of giving her customary performance, however, she waved her fan and chanted a now-celebrated love song praising the virtues of her lover and lamenting the fate that had torn them asunder, ending her ballad with the anticipation of the joys of her reunion with him. It became the most famous song-and-dance in Japanese history.

Normally, according to the morality of her time and the character of Yoritomo, she would immediately have been put to death for such an act of defiance. However, her beauty and uncommon courage struck a note of admiration from Lady Masako, the woman who was soon to wield immense powers as the matriarch of Kamakura after her husband's death. She intervened to save Shizuka's life.

Lady Shizuka was discovered to be pregnant. She was

detained in prison until the baby, Yoshitsune's child, was born. This unluckily proved to be a son, so Yoritomo ordered the infant to be left to die by the seaside. Shizuka herself was permitted to disappear into obscurity.

Yoritomo's two sons, Yoriie and Sanetomo, succeeded him in turn, and each met with violent death. The murder of Sanetomo was particularly treacherous and bizarre. Only twenty-eight at the time, he was by nature a poet rather than politician, and ill-equipped to be shogun. The night of January 27, 1219, was wild and stormy, with snow two feet deep on the ground, when Sanetomo made his way to the Hachiman Shrine to give thanks for an honor received from the emperor. He was accompanied by a retinue of high officials and a thousand cavalrymen, but he ordered the procession to remain in the courtyard as, followed by a single attendant, he entered the shrine to pray. He refused to heed the advice of his councillors, who urged him to postpone the ceremony until the daylight hours, and to wear armor under his robes of state. Apparently Sanetomo had a presentiment that he was about to die, for it was later discovered that he had written a poem before departing for the shrine, addressing it to a plum tree in his yard, asking it not to forget to bloom in the spring even though he, the lord of the household, would not be present.

As Sanetomo descended the long stairway of Hachiman Shrine following the ceremony, a shadowy figure, disguised in woman's garb, rushed out from behind the giant gingko tree near the foot of the stairs. The malevolent plotter was his own nephew Kugyo, a youth who had become demented by the assassination of his father Yoriie and his own failure to succeed him as shogun. Before the startled retainers were aware of what was taking place, Kugyo succeeded in decapitating Sanetomo with his sword and escaping into the night. As the common telling of the episode has it, he carried Sanetomo's severed head under his arm as he fled, later flinging it away. The spot where the head is reputed to have landed has been set off by a picket fence and a marker by the memorial-loving Japanese. Kugyo was later captured and killed.

With the deaths of Sanetomo and Kugyo, Yoritomo's line became extinct, and the rule of Kamakura was taken over by the Hojo family, led by Yoritomo's widow, Lady Masako. A remarkable woman, she is known to history as the Nun Shogun, for she took the tonsure after her husband's death. Although never actually a shogun herself, hers was the dominant influence of the time, exercised both through her sons Yoriie and Sanetomo and after their deaths. When the retired emperor Gotoba declared war on Kamakura in 1221, Lady Masako addressed her generals with a ringing appeal for pride and unity. Under her authority a vast army was raised, which roundly defeated the enemy from Kyoto. Her death came shortly after, in 1225 when she was sixty-eight years old, but until then she ruled Kamakura with stern justice.

The heyday of the Kamakura epoch lasted only 141 years, a brief span of time as history goes. The end came when the loyalist forces under Nitta Yoshisada were hurled against the city in three divisions, and Kamakura was wiped out. July 5, 1333 was a day of unbelievable carnage. The defenders, headed by the regent Hojo Takatoki together with nearly eight-hundred followers, committed suicide by hara-kiri when defeat seemed inevitable. More than six thousand others later followed suit, so unwavering were they in loyalty to their leader. Their graves are still marked and their memory recalled among the silent hills of Kamakura.

And over the whole region, the Great Buddha extends a benediction that touches all who have the heart to hear the voice of Kamakura's great past.

12

Kyoto

the Aristocratic

ONE JUNE NIGHT, GENERATIONS AGO, WHEN the city of Kyoto was bathed in the serene light of a full summer moon, a burly giant of a man, Benkei by name, with a halberd in hand, advanced cautiously toward the Gojo Bridge. Suddenly he halted, arrested by the sweet strains of a flute. Soon there appeared a comely lad about fifteen years of age. He was wearing a sword and playing a flute, filling the air with its melody.

Benkei had vowed to waylay all who might pass by, subdue them, and take their swords from them by force. His purpose was to win one thousand swords. He chuckled to himself when he saw the youth. He had already amassed 999 weapons, so the story goes, and the taking of his last sword seemed almost too easy for belief.

Benkei took no chances, however. He uttered a fearsome cry at the youthful flute player and demanded that he hand over his sword. To his surprise, the young one dared Benkei to take it from him. In fury at the insult, Benkei slashed furiously with his long blade, but he soon found to his astonishment that all his vaunted strength as a master swordsman was of no avail before the lad's skill and agility.

Vainly Benkei tried to overpower his opponent, but the youth eluded every blow, and Benkei's halberd cut only the empty air. The burly swordsman was finally forced to beg for mercy, dropping in exhaustion to his knees at the foot of the bridge. For all his rude exploits, he was a simple-hearted man, and he forthwith asked to become the young stranger's retainer. Such was the beginning of a friendship famous in song and history. The boy's name was Ushiwaka-maru, who later achieved renown as Yoshitsune, Yoritomo's brother and the great military hero of the Gem-pei wars of the twelfth century (see Chapters 11 and 15).

This is one of the thousand episodes that enrich the history of Kyoto, the great seat of culture on the banks of the Kamo River. Although the city is old, it was planned from its beginning in 794, when Emperor Kammu transferred his capital here from Nagaoka. Nestled in a bowl-like hollow, with hills rising around it in a semicircle, this ancient city has so many historic buildings and treasures of art as to give rise to the saying: "If you have eyes to see, go to Kyoto."

Kyoto is the ancient home of no less than 253 Shinto shrines and 1,600 Buddhist temples, as well as numerous palaces and pavilions built by emperors and feudal shogun. Some of these buildings are of massive proportions, with five-story pagodas soaring above them like sentinels in the sky.

However interesting may be the romance of Kyoto's storied past, nothing in Japanese history equals the chivalry of the gesture of the foreigner whose name is indelibly linked with the city's destiny. He was Dr. Langdon Warner. In the dark days of 1945, when the Pacific War was approaching its end, this relatively obscure scholar heard that American scientists had perfected a weapon harnessing the power of the atom, and that high strategists in the Pentagon were planning to drop it on Kyoto.

Dr. Warner immediately went to work to persuade Washington against this course, arguing that Kyoto was an open city and a cultural treasure house whose destruction would constitute an irreparable loss to mankind. His pleadings were somehow heard, and Kyoto was spared the fate of Hiroshima and Nagasaki. A statue of him now stands in neighboring Nara, another city passed over in the wartime raids because of Dr. Warner's intercession.

In olden times the area north of Sanjo was crossed by a broad river bed where the Kamo flowed among reedy banks and islands. The word Kamo means "duck," and the river received its name because of the vast flocks of waterfowl that once were found along its course. In those days Kyoto was a semi-sylvan retreat, with temples and palaces half concealed in the woods on both banks of the stream. Times have changed since those halcyon days when by law no one was allowed even to whistle lest the music of the songbirds be interrupted. Now the "thunder tribe" of wild teen-age motorcyclists roars past the once sacred groves, traveling here from as far away as Osaka and points beyond. Not only has the din frightened away the cuckoos and nightingales that enriched classical literature, but the thrushes and wrens and a thousand other creatures of the wild that once enchanted Kyoto's citizens have all but vanished.

Despite the typhoons that repeatedly lash the woods and the bulldozers that today carve ugly scars on hillsides, Kyoto is still the queen among the cities of East Asia. Here, in the old tradition of handicraft, was born the art of Nishijin brocade, which gets its name from the Nishijin quarter of the city where it was first perfected. Here too, from ancient time, are practiced the crafts of silk-weaving, embroidering, and dyeing, which enable Kyoto's citizens to clothe their ladies with some of the loveliest kimono ever devised.

For the gourmet, Kyoto is truly a happy hunting ground

where he can not only sample superb Japanese cuisine but also acquire vessels suitable for serving it. This city of fine taste is also the center of a notable ceramics industry. Its Kiyomizu and Awata ware, flourishing since the seventeenth century, are known wherever fine craftsmanship is prized.

For all its claim to fame in other fields, Kyoto, with a population of a million and a quarter, making it the fourth largest city in Japan, is still best known as the country's ancient capital. For more than a thousand years it was not only the seat of the imperial court, but the country's center of learning and art. It is richer in history, in relics, and in cultural monuments than any other Japanese city. To list even a few of its treasures is to recall the city's ancient splendor.

For instance, there is the former Imperial Palace where to this day all Japanese emperors are enthroned. First built by Emperor Kammu in 794, the original structure was destroyed by fire, as were a succession of others built afterwards. The present buildings, exact replicas of the original, date from 1855.

For the lovers of romance, there is Yasaka Shrine, built in 1654 and commonly called Gion Shrine. It was within these peaceful compounds, back in the middle of the eighteenth century, that a strange-looking young man, his face unshaven and hair ungroomed, sat on a straw mat on the ground displaying fans on which he painted pictures to attract customers. Yuri, a girl from a nearby teahouse, became intrigued by this man of Buddha-like impassiveness who sold hardly any fans but who nevertheless arrived punctually each day, rain or shine, to eke out a meager livelihood. A romance blossomed between them, but as Yuri was already married, she was determined to give her daughter, then only a little girl, as his bride. Seven years later he married the daughter.

This young man later achieved renown as the painter Ike no Taiga, considered today as the greatest Nanga-style painter of all time. His wife, Machi, the child bride whom he taught to paint, showed not only her husband's artistic brilliance but also some of his eccentricities. Carefree, careless, and endowed with rare gifts, the happy couple produced masterpiece after masterpiece in a little shack built in the precincts of another nearby shrine.

The most famous single edifice in Kyoto, of course, is the Kinkaku-ji (Golden Pavilion), erected in 1397. Much to the sorrow of antiquarians, the original structure was burned to the ground by a young Buddhist monk in 1950. Yukio Mishima, a popular literary figure, created a psychological novel based on the story of that conflagration. The three-story building, its ineffable beauty reflecting the Ashikaga shogun Yoshimitsu's sybaritic taste, was rebuilt in 1955 in an exact reproduction of the original.

Katsura Detached Palace is perhaps the most multi-faceted of Kyoto's famous landmarks. Here the fine Japanese arts of landscaping, architecture, and classical painting have been combined, in the perfection of their forms, into a single, beautiful whole. Katsura's gardens and buildings reflect the culmination of that aesthetic taste which dominated court society during Kyoto's reign as ancient capital. Within the palace rooms are contained paintings by Kano Tanyu, one of the greatest of Japanese classical painters.

The most celebrated, most photographed, most discussed of Japan's gardens lies within the precincts of Kyoto's Ryoan-ji temple, a monastery of the Rinzai sect of Zen Buddhism. This *hiraniwa* (flat garden) is a wondrous creation, composed entirely of raked white sand inset with fifteen carefully selected and positioned rocks. The sternly simple composition, with its aesthetic roots deep in the Buddhist philosophy of form and emptiness, conveys a stillness and serenity which surpasses all attempts to discuss it.

Less widely known, but cherished by many Japanese, is the first tea-ceremony room that Rikyu, patron figure of the tea cult, built for Hideyoshi. In essentially its original form, it stands today on its original site at Yamazaki, in the southern suburbs of Kyoto. Known as Tai-an, and situated within the Myoki-an temple, it is now classified as a national treasure, surely one of the most modest of all treasures. The Tai-an consists of a single room about six feet square, with a tiny entrance more like a window than a door, through which a person can enter only on his hands and knees. It was in this tiny, simple room that the gentle tea master instructed Hideyoshi, the great man of arms.

In the light of history, and by the standards of man's progress toward culture, Sen no Rikyu (1521–1591) was undoubtedly one of Kyoto's most eminent citizens. It is no accident that Rikyu, a mystic and seer, symbolizes Kyoto, whereas neighboring Osaka, a prodigious extrovert of a city, glories in Hideyoshi and his mammoth castle. The manner in which Rikyu the philosopher and Hideyoshi the conqueror became embroiled in a mortal duel forms one of the most poignant dramas out of Kyoto's colorful past.

The ritual of tea-making is very old. In a northeastern corner of Kyoto is another lovely pavilion called the Ginkaku-ji (Silver Pavilion). In it is the famous *chashitsu* (tearoom) built by Shuko (1422–1502), originator of the tea ceremony. But the man who brought this cult to its finest flowering, giving it philosophic significance, was Sen no Soeki, better known by the court name of Rikyu. He was an intellectual, a scholar with a solid background of Buddhist learning.

Without delving into the intricacies of Zen Buddhism, on which *cha-no-yu* (tea ceremony) is based, or into the concepts of *wabi* and *sabi* as the primary tenets of Japanese aestheticism, it is sufficient here to say that Rikyu possessed, to a high degree, that sense of inner serenity and self-discipline which is the basis of the philosophy of the tea ceremony. All the elaborate rituals that go with the tea ceremony

214

—the tasting of the tea, the precise motions and silences, the exchange of compliments, the contemplation of nature —are but the outward trappings of the will to master oneself, to free oneself from the futile desires and vanities that dominate man throughout his life.

In *cha-no-yu,* the house of ritual, or tea-room, is small, simple, and spotlessly clean. It is not merely a place for drinking tea; it is a place for chaste thoughts and chaste living. It is a sanctuary of tranquility—a place to lose oneself, and thus gain life, in the manner of all great religions.

Not only did Rikyu preach his doctrine, but he practised it himself with relentless austerity. And still, in the end, he proved to be only a mortal, a man susceptible to the consequences of other men's vanities; he was tragically caught in the toils of Hideyoshi's terrible animosities, from which death was the only escape.

There were three main causes for the break in the friendship between the two men. Briefly these were as follows:

Rikyu had a fair daughter, Ginko by name, who had already been widowed by the death of her "husband." In point of fact, however, she had merely been betrothed to the man, but Ginko in the old tradition of marital fidelity had sworn to live a "widow's life," and be true to the memory of her man. It was about this time that Ginko's lovely figure caught Hideyoshi's eye. In his impulsive manner, he forthwith proposed that he "favor" her by accepting her as one of his many handmaidens, a course which proud old Rikyu resolutely opposed.

Also, Rikyu had carved a wooden statue of himself in the likeness of a commoner wearing humble clothes and mean straw sandals, and he deposited his handiwork in the top gallery of the Sanmon temple gate of Daitoku-ji in the city of Sakai. Hideyoshi considered this an act of great audacity, even impudence, since such august personages as the emperor, or Hideyoshi himself, might pass on foot right under the image on their way to worship.

The third cause of enmity between the two was the unconfirmed rumor that Rikyu had accepted bribes from curio dealers in exchange for making false estimates of objects of art, thus helping to swindle the public "for the sake of a few miserable coins." Sharp charges were made that the old master, in the guise of high arbiter of art, called "priceless objects trumperies, and cheap imitations genuine articles." Hideyoshi himself joined in the fray, calling Rikyu's action treasonable.

Ostensibly because of these three matters, Hideyoshi demanded that Rikyu commit hara-kiri. The charges seem hardly to warrant such a drastic command.

In the first place, Hideyoshi's infatuation and his insistence upon acquiring Rikyu's daughter by force if necessary added no luster to his acquisitive person. A man of loose morals in loose times, he already had numerous wives, many of them daughters of famous generals and daimyo. One girl more or less in his harem was nothing to ruffle the equanimity of this man of the world, and he could therefore well have afforded to leave the proud girl alone.

As regards the second charge, it was suggested at the time that the offending statue be quietly removed and the incident forgotten. Such a course would have been infinitely more appropriate to the image Hideyoshi sought for himself as a magnanimous statesman. Instead, he stubbornly made an issue of the incident, much to the detriment of his great name.

Finally, there was some question about whether the third charge was actually true, although Rikyu himself once had declared in his offhand manner that "even a piece of common bamboo, if made into a teaspoon by the hand of a master of the tea ceremony, may thereby acquire a high moral value far above its monetary price." As a matter of fact, he may have made some bluntly unconventional judgements on *objects d'art* since he was himself an unconventional man, but it is hard to believe that such an unworldly person had accepted bribes.

216

One observer analyzed the situation in these words: "The truth probably is that it was not Rikyu's refusal of Ginko but the way that refusal was made, not the 'treasonable acts' themselves but the unbending, steely pride behind his subservient exterior that mortally offended the Taiko."

What kind of man was Hideyoshi, then? Physically a small man, hardly five feet tall, he had great verve and audacity, as well as wrath like thunder. He was bold, aggressive, cruel, magnanimous, crafty, shrewd, vain, and remarkably astute. His personality was an inscrutable contradiction, as fascinating as any figure out of fiction.

This wizard of the battlefield knew both how to fight, and how to avoid a fight. Skillful as a general in the techniques of mobility and surprise, he also knew how to win over an enemy without fighting, either by flattery, bluster, stratagem, or magnanimity. He was civilized, and he was barbaric. He was a princely playboy, full of wit and drollery, but he was also a wise administrator, giving peace to his people and order to his country where there had been only chaos before.

He was a good performer of *kyogen* (comic drama), and something of a connoisseur of the arts, of tea ceremony, architecture, painting, and poetry. He had no great talent himself but he knew how to take advice from the men around him who were truly artists, some of them of great renown. This was a priceless attribute for the nation's dictator to possess in a time of great prosperity and artistic affluence.

Hideyoshi built great castles, elegant palaces, vast temples. He may not have been the most magnificent patron in history, but his name inevitably recalls the splendors of the Medici and Pericles. Like them he produced a great age. His Momoyama epoch was as dazzling for his country as Pericles' epoch was for Greece. His scale of living was fabulous, for he requisitioned the services of the country's best architects, artists, sculptors, performers, scholars. Under his lavish patronage, the arts flourished, people prospered, and the paintings of his time became a synonym for a grandeur of style such as had never before been seen in his country.

In the end, however, it was vanity that unmade him. He sought to emulate the great Kublai Khan, whose empire two centuries earlier had stretched from the Pacific to the Danube. So Hideyoshi dispatched an expeditionary force, in the manner of conquerors from Alexander to Napoleon. He wanted to subdue Korea and the Middle Kingdom (China). And there, on the continent, his dream collapsed as his generals became mired in the endless stretches of Asia.

What perhaps most rankled Hideyoshi at the time of his quarrel with Rikyu was that he was regarded in certain indiscreet circles as a rustic, largely because of his peasant origin. He was, however, nobody's fool. He had agents quietly gathering intelligence, and he was aware of the whispers that went the rounds surreptitiously at his expense.

Although a military genius, he was no aesthete, much less a poet. In the realm of *cha-no-yu* and the other arts, he never acquired complete mastery. But human nature being what it is, Hideyoshi liked to fancy himself precisely what he was not. All the glories he had acquired in war were not enough. To his way of thinking, he had won an empire, and now it was time for him to relax a bit, and swagger a little, and dawdle with the elite of his time as a fancier of *cha-no-yu*. This was a most beguiling state of affairs, save that not all shared his illusions, especially Rikyu.

To a man of taste like Rikyu, whose whole life was dedicated to beauty in all fields of human endeavor, the spectacle of this energetic extrovert posing as a high priest of culture must have been disconcerting, all the more so because he was forced by the circumstance of Hideyoshi's authority to be at the dictator's beck and call as his chief ceremonial officer.

Rikyu was older by fifteen years than Hideyoshi. When their fatal differences occurred, the tea master was already seventy, while Hideyoshi at fifty-five was in the prime of his powers. Rikyu had been befriended by their common lord Oda Nobunaga ten years before Hideyoshi became all-powerful. Thus the two men had once been equals as fellow vassals in the service of a common master, but now Hideyoshi ruled all Japan. Although Rikyu was revered as the first name in the kingdom of taste, this was not enough in itself to soften the sense of power the warlord held over him or to make his position more bearable.

Most Japanese authorities are now inclined to believe that Hideyoshi had merely wished to crush Rikyu's proud heart, not to kill him, and that he might have pardoned him if only the older man had made some contrite gesture seeking forgiveness.

Rikyu had many friends, some of them in high places. They all advised him, even begged him, to use the good offices of Lady Kita no Kata, Hideyoshi's first wife, who was the only person the Taiko might have listened to in such a case. The lady's intercession was available, but Rikyu refused to ask for it. With his Oriental mysticism, the great saint of the tea cult chose death before surrender, and he deliberately proceeded to carry out his choice with all the stoicism of a soldier.

Adversity was nothing new for Rikyu, both as an experience and as a doctrine. He had long preached the ideal of *jaku* (loneliness or adversity). All his life he had propounded the creed of poverty and austerity.

On the morning of February 28, 1592, he rose early as usual. Outside, while the dew was still on the grass, he gathered some rape flowers. Arranging them in his favorite vase, he placed them in an alcove in his tea-room. Next he made some ceremonial tea, with his wife and a few intimates for company. He served and drank the tea according to the ritual he had perfected. Then he wrote a poem:

> What a lucky man you are, Rikyu.
> You are to become a Kanshojo.

(Kanshojo was the posthumous title of Sugawara Michizane. He was a martyred scholar of the tenth century who has since been deified, and shrines in various Japanese cities dedicated to his memory attract pilgrims to this day who worship him as Tenjin-sama, god of learning.)

When these quiet gestures were completed, he attached paper labels bearing the names of his friends to the most valued of his tea utensils which he intended as his parting gifts. He left one teabowl for himself, however. From this he drank his last cup of tea. Then he broke it to fragments, just before he ended his life by the prescribed rituals of hara-kiri, thus returning his soul to the timeless peace of Lord Buddha.

Rikyu was buried within the compounds of Daitoku-ji temple in Kyoto, where to this day followers of the tea cult make their pilgrimages. The granite tombstone above his grave is believed to have been brought from Korea during Hideyoshi's expedition to that country. In the center of it is a round hollow, which gives out a faint sound like the sighing of water simmering in the kettle used for the tea ceremony he loved so much.

Thus Rikyu died as he lived, a great man of culture in the true tradition of Kyoto, Japan's most beautiful, most aristocratic, city.

13

Nara

An Epoch Like
a Cup of Wine

> Do not waste time
>   with fruitless thoughts—
> Better to forget them
>   with a potent draught of wine.

This is the first stanza of *The Song of Sakè* which the poet
Otomo no Tabito composed in the eighth century in praise
of the god of wine. The work was written at a time when
culture reached its fullest flowering in Nara, the ancient
Japanese capital which predated Kyoto.

Tabito lived in the same century as Li Po, his Chinese
counterpart who also wrote in praise of the joys of wine.
The Japanese poet came before Li Po, and he was older by
several centuries than either Omar Khayyam or Francois
Villon, both also renowned for poems celebrating the
pleasures of drinking. Of these four singers of bacchanalian

hymns, the Japanese was the most versatile, since his fame rests upon his accomplishments not only as a poet but also as a statesman, *bon vivant,* and military leader.

It was characteristic of the age of Nara that the cultured whole man was held in higher esteem than the brilliant specialist. Nara's citizens admired men whose talents embraced the arts of both war and peace. The soldier, in those times, was also a poet. By day he fought battles against the "barbarians" on the far frontiers of the realm. By night he composed poetry. He cherished beauty because, for him, it was the only permanent thing in a transitory world. It was no mere coincidence that some of the finest poems of the Nara period were written by soldiers.

A visitor to Nara today is likely to be struck chiefly by the fact that its ancient landmarks are not castles but temples, not fortresses but Buddhist images, some of them of heroic size. The plain of Yamato where Nara is located was the cradle of Japan, and the temple grounds of Horyu-ji in Nara represent the culmination of the earliest phase of its civilization. Horyu-ji is not a single edifice but a whole collection of buildings of rare beauty, whose curved roofs and dream-like pagoda still rise above the pines like a lovely vision. The temple is very old, dating back to the seventh century. It is the oldest wooden structure extant anywhere in the world.

The man most closely associated with this phase of Nara's history was Shotoku Taishi (573–621), the illustrious prince regent who carried out many far-reaching social reforms, including promulgation of a constitution. But the Nara age proper, as distinguished from the earlier period of Nara culture, began auspiciously under an empress.

The year 708 was notable in Japanese annals because copper was discovered in the Chichibu Mountains near what is now Tokyo. Two years later the imperial court was moved to Nara from an older capital on the southern Yamato Plain. The two events were related.

In the history of most early cultures, copper was generally used for making weapons for use in tribal wars. In Nara it was reserved almost exclusively for coinage and for creating Buddhist images, reliquaries, and temple bells. The metal was prized so highly by the reigning empress Gemmei that she was moved to proclaim a new era name in honor of its discovery. She also took the occasion to transfer her capital by imperial decree. An ancient record states that the new capital "blossomed out like sweet-smelling flowers," so fair was the new location at the foot of Mt. Mikasa.

Nara, even to this day, is a haven of tranquility and natural beauty. It has woodlands, ponds, grassy knolls, and parks where tame deer roam freely. In its early period, the city, which enjoyed imperial patronage, extended over an area many times its present limits. It boasted handsome buildings supported by massive pillars and white walls. These were decked with soaring tile roofs. Here were administrative offices, palaces, and huge temples by the score. The ruling aristocracy lived in mansions that were constructed on stone foundations of a size that amazes antiquarians today as an indication of the richness of life in Nara more than a thousand years ago.

The Nara era was also one of high imperial prestige. The monarchs wielded an absolute authority such as was never exercised before or since. They both reigned and ruled, in contrast to later years when the real power was usurped by military dictators and the emperor left a powerless figurehead.

The culture that flowered in Nara was tinged with the gentle doctrine of Buddhism. The age was largely dominated by female rulers, for not always has Japan been a man's world, and especially not during the Nara era. In the brief seven decades of the era, no fewer than four empresses ruled, one of them ascending the throne for a second time after an interval. Under feminine rule Nara was a place of peace and great artistic development. Warlike activities were confined to the lonely, distant outposts. Within the capital it-self, a religious fervor pervaded the atmosphere, soon spreading over the entire land. The arts flourished, and poetry entered a golden age. The temples of the time were a combination of university and museum, as well as places of worship. As seats of learning, they not only housed great works of sculpture and painting, but also became guardians of the performing arts, including music and dancing.

Nara's wealthy families vied with one another in building yet bigger and more stately temples, whose remains still dot the landscape in the environs of the city. Happily for posterity, the rulers themselves set the style for patronage of the arts. Emperor Tenji, for instance, made contribu-tions to the Sufuku-ji temple, Temmu the Daikan Dai-ji temple, and Jito the Yakushi-ji temple. The Horyu-ji temple was burned down completely during Tenji's reign, but it was later rebuilt by Empress Gemmei, who lavished the wealth and labor of the nation on its construction. This is the famous Horyu-ji that still stands today.

Yakushi-ji rises imposingly to the west of present-day Nara. With its three-storied pagoda piercing the sky like a jewel-tipped spear, this magnificent structure was the special creation of Empress Gensho.

Despite the prominence of female rulers in this period, the most lasting monument to Nara was created, not by a woman, but by a man. He was Emperor Shomu, the Con-stantine of Japan, who was the moving spirit behind the project to build Nara's colossal image of Buddha. So big is the statue, towering seventy-one feet above the bronze pedestal on which it is seated, that the viewer's first impres-sion is one of astonishment. It is housed in a temple 155 feet high. Local wits like to tweak tourists' credulity with boasts that one can climb right up into the Buddha's nostril with an umbrella spread open. Legend has it that Ishikawa

Goemon, Japan's most notorious outlaw, once lived inside the right nostril of the statue when he was in hiding from the law before being finally caught and boiled alive in a huge kettle as punishment for his crimes. These fanciful tales are an exaggeration, of course, but they seem almost believable when one is confronted, for the first time, with the Buddha's vast size.

Emperor Shomu, one of the more astute rulers during Japan's long history, was a devout man. As the young Crown Prince Sakurahiko, he had bided his time during the reigns of two empresses before he attained his majority and ascended the throne in 724. His reign was marked by incessant incursions in the north by fierce Ainu tribesmen, whom he finally repelled with a great show of force.

In Nara, Shomu became known as a great builder. He was a monarch with expansive ideas and the necessary powers to put them into execution. After a period of meditation, he decided to create something strikingly symbolic of his faith in Buddha. As champion of his faith, Shomu issued an edict mobilizing the resources of the state for building the Great Buddha. It was to be for him, as it were, a candle lit in a dark world in divine supplication for the blessings of his people. His prayer was a plain one offered in a humble spirit, but there was nothing plain about his ideas for the mammoth monument.

Before undertaking this project, Shomu held council with his ministers and prominent citizens. Some of them opposed it as being too costly a burden for his people to bear, but Shomu overruled them. He then obtained huge supplies of copper from Kyushu and silver from the island of Tsushima. About this time gold deposits were discovered in what is now Miyagi, but because their output was not enough to fill his needs he imported additional gold from Korea. This precious metal he used chiefly to gild the statue.

Kuninaka no Muraji Kimmaro, an engineer, was commissioned to supervise the fashioning of the giant image.

He first devised a wooden crib upon which was placed the clay mold. Then he put over this a slab of white wax, and this in turn was covered with another layer of clay. When the molten bronze was poured into the waxen layer, the hot metal melted the wax and filled out the space by force of gravity. Eight different castings were required to complete the task.

All the high dignitaries of the time, led by Emperor Shomu himself and his consort, attended the ceremonies celebrating the completion of the mold in 746. Fifteen thousand candles were burned in a high mass, and participants in priestly robes prayed till midnight amid chantings and the solemn tolling of bells.

The casting required four more years, and celebrations marking completion of both the temple and the Buddha took place on April 9, 752. By then, some fifty tons of copper and eight tons of pewter had been used. Emperor Shomu, who had by then gone into religious retirement, accompanied the Empress Koken, his successor, to this celebration. Ten thousand priests gathered to witness the ceremony of painting the eyes of the Buddha, a ritual which symbolized completion of the image and entry of the divine spirit into the Buddha's bronze body.

By all accounts, this original Buddha was a superb work of art. Unfortunately for posterity, it suffered a series of mishaps in the subsequent twelve hundred years of its existence which all but ruined its once ineffable beauty. Around the year 820 an earthquake shook the image so violently that its head rolled to the ground. The headless Buddha remained mercilessly untended for the next forty-two years before it was restored.

In 1180 the temple housing the Buddha was destroyed by fire. In the conflagration, both the head and right hand melted off, presenting a sad sight to holy pilgrims who continued to worship before the defaced relic. Ex-emperor Goshirakawa, in 1185, had the image restored, celebrating this restoration with great pomp and ceremony.

In the civil war of 1556, the temple was again gutted by fire, and again the head melted. A wooden face was devised as a substitute and covered with sheets of copper to give it a semblance of its original bronze appearance, but the work was not successful. In those troubled times there was not enough zeal or resources among the people to restore the temple sheltering it, and so the poor Buddha was left to the mercy of the elements for the next 140 years. Then a remarkable zealot, the chief abbot of Todai-ji, undertook to rebuild the temple and repair the figure. By 1692 the statue's wooden head had been replaced by one fashioned of real bronze.

The statue suffered further damage from time to time, as the afflictions of old age caused the Buddha to sag here and bend there under its immense weight. This necessitated installment of buttresses, which in those early times had to be fashioned without benefit of steel or concrete. They were never completely successful. By this time, the great age of sculpture had long since passed, and the wondrous beauty of the original image, a fit theme for song and poetry down through the ages, could never be restored.

The last repairs were made on the head, chest, hands, and other parts of the image in the Edo era. By these poorly executed alterations the statue was finally bereft of its original timeless grace and serenity, and in their place appeared the harsh line of decadence. Scholars to this day speculate on the Buddha's original beauty by carefully appraising those parts that still remain as originally created, including the pedestal and the flowing lines of the Buddha's garment. By such means they have concluded that this great dream of Emperor Shomu must have been fashioned on a standard of art comparable to that of some of the small but precious specimens of glyptic art still preserved from the same period.

These give us some idea of what mankind lost when Nara's great Buddha was repeatedly mutilated by the elements and inept repairs.

⊛

Not all historical figures of Nara were statesmen, priests, or emperors. There was, for instance, Abe no Nakamaro, Japan's most celebrated expatriate.

In its heyday, cultural ties between Nara and the Chinese imperial capital at Changan were at a high tide. At frequent intervals, missions consisting of as many as five hundred persons or more were sent abroad to exchange goods and acquire learning from the neighboring continental power, which was then prospering under the brilliant T'ang dynasty. Ancient documents tell of expeditions consisting of ambassadors, physicians, priests, and scholars.

Travel abroad in those days was an adventure. Embassies braved the hazards of travel in sailing ships that were often scattered by storm or waylaid by pirates. If all went well, the emissaries stayed in the friendly kingdom for varying lengths of time before returning with Chinese learning on such diverse subjects as theology, architecture, engineering, arts and crafts, and literature. Some of these envoys won great fame, not only in Japan but in China itself, where they met with the leading figures of the imperial court. Nakamaro was one of these.

An ambitious lad, he had set out for the Celestial Kingdom at the age of seventeen. Records show that he was one of 550 persons making the voyage. Fortunately for him he acquired a friend at the Chinese court, who was none other than the Emperor Hsuan-tung himself, a kindly soul who was attracted by the youth's personable nature and encouraged his considerable talents. His Majesty finally appointed him a high court functionary with the rank of minister.

Nakamaro's years in China slipped by like a dream as

his fame as a poet spread far and wide. In the company of bosom companions, he whiled away his days pleasantly, penning verses and engaging in witty conversations with the best minds of the age. Then, when he was nearing fifty-three, unbearable nostalgia assailed him, and this Japanese Marco Polo suddenly decided to revisit his native Nara.

It was probably at Chekiang that he composed the single poem that has made him immortal. In this verse he sang of his attachment for the Kasuga Shrine of his boyhood that nestled in the green plain of Nara. The poem has been preserved for more than a thousand years in the collection known as *One Hundred Poems by One Hundred Poets*. It reads:

> I look up, and there in the sky
> Appears the self-same moon
> That rises out of
> Mt. Mikasa above Kasuga of my homeland.

After composing the little verse for posterity, Nakamaro left for home, but he was shipwrecked on the way. Set adrift on a stormy sea, he finally found haven in a seaside village of Chinese Annan. Eventually, after much hardship wandering about in a famous Oriental Odyssey, the sentimental traveler returned to Changan. Although he lived for nearly another score years, and finally died when he was seventy, he never again saw his native land.

The Nara era was Japan's golden age of poetry. Its *Manyoshu* or *Collection of a Myriad Leaves* is an anthology containing more than four thousand poems arranged in twenty volumes. They were written, for the most part, around the time when Li Po and Tu Fu were adding luster to Chinese poetry and the Beowulf epic was coming to life in the West.

The earlier poems of the *Manyoshu* fall in the reign of Emperor Nintoku (313–99) and the last one is dated 799.

It is certain, however, that most of these tiny, terse, imagistic poems were composed in the hundred years before 760. These are robust creations springing from diverse levels of society. Their authors range from emperors and courtiers down to foot soldiers, peasants, and maids. Read today after a lapse of so many centuries, these lyrics still seem strangely fresh and compelling.

Many poems in the *Manyoshu* were composed by soldiers far from home guarding the frontiers against hostile tribesmen. On many a lonely night, as they took up station under the stars, they composed poems to while away their tedium. One such a poet-soldier was Tajihi. Thinking of his wife back home, he wrote these words.

> Calling overhead, cranes fly
> to the reedy shores.
> I am desolate and lonely
> as I sleep alone!

There was also Lady Kasa, a talented woman in the service of the imperial court. In love with a court official far above her station, she wrote these dancing words of love:

> How fully do I love thee—
> Though you awe me like the waves
> thunderously lashing the seacoast of Ise.

Like the poetess Yosano Akiko of a thousand years later, Lady Kasa was also a woman who sang of the untamed emotions in her heart with great eloquence. She wrote:

> If, as they say, it is death to love—
> Then have I died, and died again,
> A thousand times over.

About the time Emperor Shomu was building his **Dai-butsu** and the streets of Nara sounded with the joyous tolling of temple bells, a poet was composing a love poem

to his beloved. His name was Otomo no Yakamochi, son of
Otomo no Tabito, whose poem was quoted at the beginning
of this chapter. In a verse familiar to every Japanese, he
described an experience still familiar to the human race:

> Forlorn with love,
>   I waste and waste away—
> I who once believed myself
>   to be a manly man!

Yamanoue Okura was another hapless lover, who
unburdened his heart in this fashion:

> Though I find this world
>   full of grief and shame,
> I cannot fly away—
>   I am not a bird.

The recurring themes of this ninth-century anthology
are love in all its aspects, fealty to lord, nostalgia for home,
and beauty of nature. As conjured up by modern readers,
the world of the *Manyoshu* appears across the distance of a
thousand years as a purer, cleaner, more heroic age, but this
is an illusion. The people of ancient Nara were much like
people everywhere, and a reading of their poems seems to
make them in fact our kin and neighbors across the distance
of time. In 699, a "girl of Suminoe," as she is described,
was presented to Prince Naga, presumably the fourth son
of Emperor Temmu, and from her relation with her lord
come these lines of rare beauty:

> Had I known before, my lord,
>   of the journey you would make,
> I would have dyed a robe for you
>   with red clay from the river banks.

An earlier anthology known as the *Kokashu*, later incor-
porated into the *Manyoshu*, contains this song of affection
and old age in Naniwa (ancient name for Osaka):

> Like the huts where Naniwa folk
> Make their fires of the river reeds,
> My wife too grows old, is becoming decrepit,
> And yet she appears always fresh to me.

It is fitting that this story of Nara should begin and end with a poem. Tabito, whose *Song of Sakè* was quoted at the beginning, worked himself up from the ranks to become a high minister of junior rank. He also served as minister of war, commander in chief of an expeditionary army, and governor general of a colony. But it was as a poet that he achieved greatest fame.

It is recorded that Li Po, his Chinese contemporary, having imbibed too freely, drowned when he jumped into a river trying to embrace the moon, whose outline was reflected in the water. Tabito, on the other hand, died a prosiac death in his sixty-seventh year, exactly thirty-one years before the unveiling of the Daibutsu. Another stanza of his *Song of Sakè* may be appropriate to end our story of Nara, for it gives an insight into the mood of an era when life was relatively simple, with its unaffected joys, a few tears, and forgetfulness in a bowl of wine.

> If, among the pleasures of the world,
> you still know sorrow,
> Then you should drink, and drink
> until the tears appear.

67. Main gate of Kofuku-ji, "Temple of the Revival of Happiness." In its heyday of influence and prosperity, this temple embraced more than 150 buildings.

Nara . . .

▲ 68

68. Kofuku-ji's five-storied pagoda, reflected in Sarusawa Pond. Designated an Important Cultural Property, this second highest pagoda in Japan was first built in 730, and ravaged by fire on five separate occasions. The present structure was erected in 1426.

69. Main pavilion of Horyu-ji, the oldest existing temple in Japan and the oldest wooden building in the world. It was founded in 607 by Shotoku Taishi.

▲ 70

▼ 71

▲ 72

70. Tame deer are numerous in the 1,250-acre Nara Park.

71. Attendants at Kasuga Shrine.

72. Daibutsu, the Great Buddha of Todai-ji, largest bronze statue in the world.

73. One of the "Twelve Divine Generals" enshrined at Shinyakushi-ji.

Osaka . . .

▲ 74

74. Osaka Castle. When Hideyoshi built this fortress in 1584, he regarded it as impregnable. Tokugawa Ieyasu, however, succeeded in destroying it in 1615, largely through subterfuge. The present structure was rebuilt in 1931, replete with elevator.

75. Yodogimi, consort of Hideyoshi, made this bridge her gift to the garden of Sumiyoshi Shrine.

76. Modern steel span across the Yodo River. Because of its many bridges and canals, Osaka is sometimes called the Venice of Japan.

▲ 75

▼ 76

▲ 77

▲ 78

▼ 79

▲ 80

▼ 81

77–81. Bunraku, the Japanese puppet theater which became renowned through the genius of Chikamatsu Monzaemon.

Kobe . . .

82–83.   Japan's largest port, her most productive shipyards. War-time raids almost completely destroyed Kobe's industry. Since that time the city has made a remarkable recovery, establishing itself in the vanguard of Western technology.

▼ 82

◀ 83

▲ 84

84. The beach at Mai-
ko; its black pines are centuries old, and famous for
their weathered forms.

85. Minatogawa Shrine,
dedicated to the patriot
Kusunoki Masashige.

85 ▶

86. A veil of mist softens the outlines of a Buddhist temple
emerging out of Nagasaki's storied past.

Nagasaki...

▲ 87

▼ 88

▲ 89

▼ 90

87. Marked Chinese in-
fluence, such as in this
gate, pervades the city.

88. Glover House,
which legend associates
with *Madame Butterfly*.

89. Cathedral of Ura-
gami, regarded as one of
the finest Christian cathedrals in the Orient.

90. The statue marks
the spot where, on August
9, 1945, the atomic bomb
fell and almost completely
destroyed Nagasaki and
its people.

91.   Dragon float in the annual Okunchi Festival.

14

Osaka

Puppets and a Castle's Fall

SPRAWLED LIKE A GIGANTIC OCTOPUS ACROSS the broad delta of the Yodo River, the city of Osaka dominates a lush plain, a symbol of wealth and ceaseless energy. It heaves and surges and grows continuously. It is forever pushing out its vast tentacles, spreading them over satellite cities. It is an ugly, nervous, roaring metropolis. It is also one of the world's great workshops.

Crisscrossed by an intricate system of canals, Osaka is bounded on two sides by ranks of mountains marching northward all the way to Lake Biwa. To the south is Osaka Bay, an expanse of water warmed by the life-giving Black Current which sweeps up from the tropics. Osaka and the Yodo River have always had an inseparable affinity. Even when the city was only a fishing hamlet, it was watered by the Yodo. The river flows with sparkling clarity out of Lake

Biwa, forty miles away, but as it crosses the fertile plain it turns muddy with the accumulation of sediment and waste of civilization. As it approaches Osaka, it becomes one vast turgid flow.

Osaka, with a population of three million, is the second largest city in Japan after Tokyo. Easterners call it the Modern Baghdad on the Yodo, testifying to its antiquity and the prosperity of its commerce, but Westerners more usually call it the Chicago of the Orient. Its productive capacities are prodigious. The city is a living organism, a breathing creature, ceaselessly in the throes of creation. It is forever making things, from tiny diodes the size of a pinhead, to cranes that lift whole locomotives and merchant ships that sail the seven seas.

Here, in the heart of the nation, forests of chimneys belch clouds of smoke. Steel furnaces blaze away day and night. Into its maw are fed raw materials from the world's four corners—lumber from the Philippines, camphor from Taiwan, cotton from Texas, wool from Australia, rice and meat from the sundry provinces of Japan. They arrive in endless streams by plane, boat, truck, and train. All the skills of man are used to fashion wares out of them. The finished products flow ceaselessly from shops, factories, and conveyor belts to markets in New York, Karachi, or Timbuctoo.

To its citizens, Osaka is a city that never sleeps. Its night life is gay, if somewhat boisterous, its restaurants are plentiful and varied, and the lights dance until dawn.

The typical Osakan has a personality all his own. His idiom is pungent, his humor uproarious. No Japanese comedy is complete without the funnyman from Osaka, with his pratfalls and comic talk. On the serious side, he follows the noble tradition of the Edo age's merchant princes. He is essentially a creature of commerce.

His city, of which he is inordinately proud, is noted for many things. Its wooded spaces are adorned with temples and shrines. Foremost among them is the Temman-gu shrine, founded in 949 and dedicated to Sugawara Michizane, patron saint of learning. Its celebrated festival, attracting enormous crowds each year in July, is highlighted by a procession of decorated boats that float down the Yodo like fairy palaces.

Equally impressive is the Shitenno-ji temple, an ancient group of buildings that includes a dream-like pagoda reaching out to the sky. This was founded in the year 593 by Shotoku Taishi, the saintly statesman known to every Japanese schoolboy as the Prince of Japanese Civilization. At regular intervals, the temple's great bell tolls solemnly, sounding a benediction from this sanctuary within a modern city. It is a sound that comes out of the past, a thousand years and more, to lay a soothing hand on man's tired soul. Even Shitenno-ji, however, is surpassed in antiquity by Osaka's Sumiyoshi Shrine, which is sacred to four Shinto deities and has a history of seventeen hundred years.

No less than the shrines and temples, the city's fast-changing skyline warms the heart of every Osaka citizen. Historical edifices remind him of past glories, but the new multi-storied ferroconcrete buildings tell him of today's prosperity.

However gratifying these visible signs may be to his sense of well being, there are four other things that never fail to stir the pride of the Osaka citizen. These are the city's ancient origin, the genius of Chikamatsu Monzaemon, the Buraku Doll Theater, and the great Osaka Castle.

Osaka is very old. In the dim past of the seventh century B.C., so it is told, the first emperor, Jimmu Tenno, went on a barbarian-subduing expedition from his base in Kyushu, landing in Naniwa (present Osaka) at the head of a band of warriors. Naniwa was then inhabited by primitive tribesmen known as Tsuchigumo (Earth Spiders), so called because they lived in caves. Jimmu conquered them, went on from there to pacify all Yamato (the plains surrounding Nara), and successfully founded the seat of his empire.

Osaka's most distinguished citizen of culture was Chikamatsu Monzaemon (1653–1724). Originally a Kyoto man, he won fame and wrote most of his masterworks while in Osaka. This literary immortal is commonly regarded as Japan's Shakespeare. As a playwright he had no peer in Japan, outshining all his contemporaries. He was born in a humble samurai family and records of his early life are spare, but when he was about thirty years old he began writing *joruri*, a kind of poetic narrative.

About the same time there appeared a brilliant reciter by the name of Takemoto Gidayu, who opened a *ningyo shibai* (doll theater) in the crowded amusement section of Dotombori. Professionally he was the Japanese counterpart of the West's medieval ballad singer. Wherever he put up shop, crowds collected, eager to be thrilled by his stirring performances. For them the inanimate dolls to which he gave voice became magically alive. Like live creatures with souls of their own, these manipulated figures strutted about, fighting and loving and dying with incredible verisimilitude. For his scripts, Gidayu used Chikamatsu's plays. This combination of the noble playwright and gifted singer developed into a rare art.

Unhappily, when Chikamatsu was sixty-two, Gidayu died. After this sad event, which grieved him greatly, Chikamatsu joined Gidayu II, the disciple who followed in his master's footsteps. Thus, for forty years Chikamatsu gave to the world masterpiece after masterpiece, mirroring the many fascinating aspects of life in the golden age of Genroku. Altogether he wrote more than one hundred pieces. Today, two and a half centuries later, his plays still move the heart.

Like all truly great artists, Chikamatsu showed compassion for his fellow men. His sense of tragedy is sometimes overwhelming, as he treats of hapless people who dance to circumstances beyond their control and starkly meet disaster with the stoicism of their age. His pity embraces not merely the socially innocent but also offenders against the law who are moved to thievery, mayhem, and murder by inexorable forces of circumstance.

Chikamatsu was also a master in the use of everyday idiom to etch out character with extraordinary clarity. The whole range of his characters, whether lovers or scoundrels, heroes or cravens, seem so vividly alive that they may well have just come out of the house next door. In his own day there was harmony of parts in the production of his plays—between the reciter's articulation and the puppeteer's gestures, between the poet's words and the music of the orchestra. This technical perfection, plus the poet's genius, laid the basis of Osaka's challenge to Edo's cultural leadership.

Chikamatsu's masterpiece is called *Kokusen ya Kassen*, A Tale from Old China, but he is better known today for the drama of double suicide called *Sonezaki Shinju*. This story is climaxed by a scene in the Sonezaki woods where the two fated lovers, their figures fitfully illuminated by lightning flashes on a thunder-rocked night, march to their death amid the mournful tolling of a temple bell. However different its outward trappings, it is a drama spiritually akin to the works of the man who penned *Macbeth* and *Romeo and Juliet*.

Chikamatsu died in 1724 in Osaka at the age of seventy-one. He is interred at Homyo-ji temple.

Out of the rich tradition nourished by Chikamatsu and Gidayu came the main outlines of the famous Bunraku Doll Theater, a unique institution now located in the Dotombori amusement section of Osaka. Designated a national treasure, the theater is the pride of Osaka. Needless to say, Chikamatsu's plays, besides being produced in *ningyo shibai*, are also performed in the live theater. Here, on the broader stage of classical Kabuki, his heroic dramas are performed to heroic proportions, and they can be seen to this day in showhouses across the country.

However interesting they may be as cultural landmarks, Chikamatsu and Bunrakuza have a potent rival for the highest position in the city's roll of honor: the castle. This moody pile of masonry dominates the city, just as the Acropolis dominates Athens. It stands solidly on a foundation of huge stone blocks, some of them fifty feet long and twenty feet high. Girded by parapets, battlements, galleries, and turreted roofs, it is crowned by a central tower where, in modern times, an elevator has been installed to take visitors to the top for a panoramic view of the whole city.

Despite its handsome appearance and its once formidable character as a fortress, the castle is an anachronism. In its day, however, it was a remarkable feat of engineering.

When completed in the sixteenth century, the castle represented a vast defensive work, a city in itself, with an outer perimeter extending seven and a half miles. It was surrounded by two lines of outer stone walls surmounted by forty-eight large watch towers and seventy-six smaller ones, all strategically located to prevent surprise assaults from every conceivable angle.

Centuries of time have crumbled the castle's warlike installations. Its innumerable buildings have been burned or destroyed, and most of the great moats were filled in, as will be shortly related, at the time of the battle of Osaka Castle (1614–15). What remains today is only a remnant of the innermost citadel. Even this is a replica, rebuilt in ferroconcrete in 1931 on the original foundation.

The original castle was built by Toyotomi Hideyoshi, who was without doubt Japan's mightiest conqueror and ablest general, though not its greatest statesman. He is sometimes referred to as the Napoleon of Japan because of his mastery of mobile war. Physically a small man, he

254

had an uncanny insight into human character. He was an inveterate plunger, full of daring and energy, but his overweening ambition finally drove him to overstep the bounds of his powers. After saving his homeland from the internecine wars that periodically laid it waste in the era before him, he gambled away his resources, including the flower of his army, in a fruitless adventure in Korea, where his generals won for him a succession of brilliant victories but lost the war.

Hideyoshi was born in 1536 in a humble peasant family near what is now the city of Nagoya. When he was seven years old, his father died. His mother remarried, and the boy was brought up by his stepfather. At fifteen the lad ran away from home, convinced that his fortunes lay elsewhere. No doubt like any other boy of his village he was fired by the thought of becoming a samurai or warrior, which entitled him to carry a sword. In the tightly compartmented caste system of his time, this was a difficult thing for a peasant boy to achieve. That he eventually succeeded and became in addition a generalissimo lording it over palace aristocrats was a measure of his mettle. One historian, describing him as a young man, gives us this picture:

Hideyoshi was "scarcely sixty inches in height, with a face as wizened as . . . a septuagenarian ape but with a supple and sinewy frame of the wiriest, that never seemed to know what fatigue was."

Early in his career, he was shrewd enough to gamble his future on the man he picked as the coming star among the many chieftains battling for power. He deliberately placed himself at the service of a little-known baron, Oda Nobunaga. His new-found patron rose quickly to primacy, making Hideyoshi his trusted liegeman.

After Nobunaga's death in battle, Hideyoshi took over. In a lightning stroke of savage fighting, he dealt a fatal blow against Akechi Mitsuhide, the usurper who had overthrown Nobunaga. Out of the struggle Hideyoshi emerged as the undisputed leader of his realm. He was a classic example of the ruthless dictator who was also capable of benevolence. It is true that he ordered the crucifixion of the celebrated twenty-six Christian martyrs in Nagasaki in 1596. Despite this and other examples of barbarism in a rough age of wars, Hideyoshi was a great stabilizing force. He gave his people peace and order and an efficient working government. He was also a great builder. In addition to Osaka Castle, he erected other notable buildings that included palaces, temples, and pavilions. Everything he did was on a colossal scale. Even his tea parties were conducted like some vast carnival, with thousands taking part in the intricate ceremonies of tea tasting.

Despite the power he wielded and the fabulous grandeur of his style of living, Hideyoshi was saddened near the close of his career by two things: the failure of his Korean campaign, where the ghosts of his stranded armies haunted him, and his uncertainty of the future of his beloved son Hideyori, who was only five when Hideyoshi died. For what it was worth, he extracted a solemn pledge from his subordinate daimyo and generals, including Ieyasu, to safeguard Hideyori's well-being. Describing the riddle of life as "a dream within a dream," he died in 1598, leaving behind Hideyori and the seeds of further struggles for power.

Hideyoshi's death paved the way for the emergence of Tokugawa Ieyasu as the next strong man. Although a subordinate daimyo under Hideyoshi, he took over the country's helm by a judicious combination of strategy and force. He finally stamped his leadership upon the reluctant daimyo by defeating an alliance of his rivals in the great battle of Sekigahara (1600).

Ieyasu first came into prominence in history some years earlier in 1590, when at the head of an army of seventy thousand men he marched into Edo, then a sleepy little fishing village nestled among reedy marshes. Here he decided to build his stronghold.

Ieyasu's boyhood had been passed in what is now Aichi prefecture. His early life was marred by brutal clan warfare, in which hostages were given and taken in primitive fashion. Out of these bitter struggles he grew to manhood with considerable military power acquired through sheer native ability.

When he was nineteen, he took for his bride a woman many years his senior. Alert to learn, and quick to adjust himself to changing conditions, he was one of the earliest daimyo to take advantage of Western firearms, a novelty in Japanese warfare. After Sekigahara, he permitted Hideyoshi's son Hideyori to keep his father's estates, including Osaka Castle, but he managed to impress unmistakably on the other daimyo his own paramount position in the land.

To cap his career, in 1603 he was granted by the emperor the title of Seii-taishogun. Although two years later he retired from the position of shogun in favor of his son Hidetada, he carefully retained all actual powers until the very end.

The struggle for power which ensued in the second decade of the seventeenth century was one of the great epics of Japanese history. It culminated in the fall of Osaka Castle after a confrontation reminiscent of the fabled Trojan War. There was the same stalemate of powerful forces, with one side entrenched in an "impregnable" castle, the other trying futilely to reduce it by force and then resorting to strategem to force its capitulation. There was also the same interplay of human factors, with blood relatives fighting against each other in the final holocaust.

Hideyori, son of the great Hideyoshi, was nineteen years old in 1612. Big and brawny, he was a full-grown man of good intentions but uncertain leadership. He was dominated by his mother Yodogimi, who goes down in history as a vain woman whose meddling cleverness lost an empire.

Around 1611, Ieyasu finally made up his mind to force a showdown with Hideyori in an attempt to stamp out the last possible traces of opposition. Since Hideyori was the rallying point of all the disgruntled elements opposed to Ieyasu's rule, Ieyasu was determined to crush him, even though Hideyori's wife was Ieyasu's own granddaughter, Princess Sen. To achieve his end Ieyasu went about his way deliberately, laying a devious trap that was slowly to undermine his rival.

The story begins some years earlier in Kyoto. There, in the Higashiyama district, the huge Hoko-ji temple and the Buddhist image of immense size which it housed were destroyed by an earthquake in 1596. In 1602, Hideyori rebuilt the temple in memory of his late father, and was in the process of casting another image to replace the original one when a fire destroyed the building. At Ieyasu's urging, Hideyori rebuilt the temple in 1612. This was a tremendous structure, towering 173 feet in the air. Four years later an immense bell was cast for it. This bell was thirteen feet tall and weighed more than forty-five tons. During ceremonies celebrating the completion of these projects, Ieyasu took false offense at an inscription written on the bell, seeing insult where none was intended. Without going into detail of the negotiations that followed to pacify the wily old statesman's ire, it is sufficient to say that the forces around Hideyori were finally convinced that Ieyasu was using the incident as an excuse to provoke war, and they girded themselves accordingly for the hostilities they judged to be unavoidable.

The war began on October 1, 1614, when Ieyasu ordered his troops to move against Osaka Castle. Despite his seventy-two years he looked fresh and spry that day as he danced on the floor, anticipating adventure and rewards. Hideyori, for his part, was overtaken with misgivings when he found that all the regional barons who were supposed to espouse his cause failed to rally to his defense.

Hideyori was disappointed, but not excessively so. The nucleus of his army was brave and in fighting trim. He was young, and the castle was strong. And he had the services of hordes of *ronin,*, masterless samurai, who had joined his cause hoping for a turn of fortune.

The battle was joined in November of 1614. This fortress that was the pride of old Hideyoshi lived up to its builder's prophecy that it could never be assaulted successfully from the outside. In his attack Ieyasu used every weapon at his command, including heavy European-type artillery, scaling gear, and battering rams. He rushed these to likely spots, pressing the attack home furiously, but to no avail. His engineers resorted to borings underground, but these efforts were also repulsed.

Stymied by Hideyori's stubborn defense, Ieyasu was in a mood to listen to overtures. These came in due time. The negotiations were prolonged and tedious. Hideyori finally agreed to have the outermost moat filled as his assurance of peaceful intentions. This was a fatal error when viewed in conjunction with the devious workings of Ieyasu's mind, which by now was bent on one aim: to crush his enemy. That Hideyori ever agreed to such a concession seems incredible, but actually he had no other recourse, since he was everywhere surrounded.

Instead of filling only the outermost moat as agreed upon, Ieyasu craftily filled in all three outer moats and then renewed the battle. Although this seriously weakened the castle's defenses, the struggle went on inconclusively through the rest of the year. Then early in 1615, Ieyasu issued an ultimatum: Hideyori must open the gates of his castle, retire to the distant province of Ise, and expel all mercenaries within the castle. Since acceptance of these conditions was tantamount to total surrender, and there was no assurance that his life and the lives of his family would be spared even if he agreed to them, Hideyori chose to fight on.

The last phase of the battle began in April. This time, since the moats had been filled in, all the fighting took place in the open. The superior numbers and resources of the attackers took a heavy toll among the defenders. Hideyori's ablest generals fell one by one in the bloody battles that took place both within and without the castle.

On May 7, street fighting broke out. Casualties were heavy on both sides, and for a while the outcome of the fighting was in the balance, so furiously and effectively did the outnumbered defenders slash their way into the enemy's ranks.

In one spectacular foray, Hideyori's famous swordsman Sanada Yukimura broke through with his men across Ieyasu's main line, invading the old general's headquarters and causing great consternation. That fateful day ended, however, with Ieyasu's men in turn penetrating the castle's inner core, and the mighty structure that was designed to endure a thousand years went up in flames that could be seen all the way to Kyoto, fifty miles away.

The final debacle, like the fall of Troy, was fraught with drama. As earlier remarked, Hideyori was married to Princess Sen, daughter of Shogun Hidetada, who acted as second in command of the enemy forces. Hidetada in turn was the son of Ieyasu, supreme commander of the attacking armies. In another way the two opposing houses were related by blood. Hidetada's wife (mother of Princess Sen) was the younger sister of Yodogimi, Hideyori's mother. Thus they were arrayed, daughter against father, sister against sister, son-in-law against father-in-law.

In one of the poignant moments of history, the lovely Princess Sen sent a messenger to her grandfather Ieyasu's camp pleading with him to spare the life of her husband Hideyori. While Ieyasu was receptive to the idea of clemency, his son Hidetada was violently opposed. A scene occurred in Ieyasu's camp during which the old general stormed in anger when Hidetada reminded him that failure to stamp out Hideyori earlier when the task was simpler had resulted in the present immense cost in bloodshed, and that clemency now for his son-in-law would only mean further bloodshed later.

As events were to prove, the hot exchange of words between the two attacking generals was meaningless, since even as they debated at their command post in the shadow of the castle, that great structure was already enveloped in flames. Hideyori and his mother Yodogimi had killed themselves as fire began eating into the inner chambers, and their bodies were consumed by flames.

Old Ieyasu was filled with anxiety over the fate of his beloved granddaughter. He quickly passed out word that anyone rescuing Princess Sen from the burning castle would be rewarded with her hand in marriage. Among the warriors who volunteered for the mission, one succeeded. He was Sakasaki Dewa no Kami. Plunging into the burning heart of the castle, he carried her out to safety. In so doing he suffered severe burns which left ugly scars.

After the battle Ieyasu made him a minor daimyo as a reward for his valor and then considered the incident closed, but not so the man who rescued the princess. Holding that a promise was a promise, he expectantly waited for fulfillment of Ieyasu's words. The spirited princess, however, spurned her rescuer's suit because, some said, the scars he had acquired in saving her life made him look ugly. Instead of becoming his bride, as expected in all good tales of heroism, she married another man. Embittered by what he considered her ingratitude, Sakasaki tried to kill her husband, but was himself slain in the attempt.

Beside the waters of Yodo the reconstructed castle of Osaka today stands moodily over the city's skyline, as if pondering the great tragedy that occurred here when the original structure was engulfed by flames that day nearly 350 years ago.

15
Kobe
Commerce and the Stuff of Legends

The lights of Moto-machi shine
    like lilies of the valley in the rain;
Dancing, dancing on the dampened asphalt
    in the rain. . . .

In these words, the popular tune *Kobe March* evokes
memories of Moto-machi, Kobe's counterpart of the famed
Ginza of Tokyo. The tune is catchy and poetic, and Moto-
machi fully merits the praise. Rain or shine, Moto-machi
acts as a magnet for the crowds sedate and fashionable
that gather here to see and be seen and to revel in the
avenue's myriad attractions. For Kobe citizens, Moto-machi
is their particular pride. Here and on Sannomiya Street
are located the main shopping districts of the city, where
visitors may obtain all sorts of goods ranging from em-
broidery and silk to curios and cameras. Kobe in turn is

Japan's greatest port, situated on Osaka Bay at the entrance to the Inland Sea.

To the north, the Rokko Mountains run east and west in wooded verdure. Parallel to them and hugging their southern flank for many miles along a narrow strip, is the city itself. Below the city is the bay, where jetties thrust out into the water, looking like the long teeth of some titan's comb stroking the white strands of the sea.

Kobe has the same dramatic qualities that have won fame for Hong Kong and San Francisco. It is built among hills, with the sea at its front and mountains at its back. It is a vast industrial center, a place where myriad factories reach all the way to Osaka. Kobe's industries are many and varied, with emphasis on textiles, steel, shipbuilding, and other heavy industries. Here are produced endless streams of rolling stock, rubber goods, locomotives, electrical goods, canned foods, and a hundred other products.

After it was thrown open to world commerce in 1868, Kobe grew to prodigious size at a prodigious rate, transforming itself from a fishing hamlet to Japan's largest port. Today it is in the vanguard of the continuing advance of Western methods and technology. In this respect it is unlike nearby Kyoto and Nara—old cities whose reputation resides almost solely in their classical heritage.

The port of Kobe, as a whole, grew from almost nothing in a few decades, although parts of the city have memories almost as old as history. Today it handles more shipping every year than Yokohama. The city slopes to the sea in an elongated sprawl of small multi-storied ferroconcrete buildings and factories. The winds that sweep down from the mountains are clean and dry, but they turn suddenly murky as soon as they strike the columns of smoke rising and spreading from the city's industrial belt.

Guarding the entrance to Osaka Bay, Kobe once served as a lair for pirates who preyed on medieval commerce. These rovers of the seas vanished with the Meiji Restoration in 1868, but something of their wild free spirit still persists among the giants of enterprise who today battle for power and keep the wheels of industry turning. Although its industries were practically wiped out by air raids during the war, Kobe has made a brilliant comeback. None of its wartime scars remain today.

After their labors, Kobe's citizens, like people everywhere, are fond of relaxing. They like to soak themselves in the steaming baths at the Arima Spa or bake their bodies in the sun at the fashionable seaside resorts of Suma or Maiko. From the spring waters at Nada, breweries make rice wine fit for the most aristocratic taste. And Kobe's beef is the rarest, most succulent item on any gourmet's list. For antiquarians the greatest point of interest in the Kobe area is the seventeenth-century Himeji Castle, which is located thirty-four miles distant and has been designated as a national treasure.

Although Yokohama was opened in 1859, it was not until nine years later that the Edo government, which was then harassed by an internal revolt, finally made Kobe an open port. In those days, Kobe, or Hyogo as it was called, was a desolate waste of sand relieved only by gnarled pines that stretched along the seashore toward Osaka. The area to the east was mostly open fields. To the west were some straw-thatched shacks where fishermen lived, and these were interspersed by a few sakè breweries and godowns. Moto-machi, where today fashion-conscious citizens parade their satorial elegance, was then a narrow and odoriferous alley lined with a jumble of huts.

The foreign traders who landed here on New Year's Day in 1868 were an odd assortment of adventurers, lured by the common expectation of easy riches. Their disillusionment was swift in coming. Housing was meager or nonexistent. A few lucky ones acquired accommodation in nearby temples, but the rest were forced to look for quarters in godowns. Before the month was over, about twenty graves had to be dug in the cemetery at Ono, where the dead were buried in plots so close to the sea that water was found at the four-foot level and the graves had to be made shallow enough to avoid the seepage. This circumstance was not lost to certain predators, both human and animal. Hungry foxes came down from the hills at night, scraping away the earth and gnawing newly buried coffins, and thieves exhumed bodies in their search for non-existent treasures they thought had been laid away with the cadavers.

In those trying days of primitive sanitation, dysentery and diphtheria took a dreadful toll, especially among the young. After the initial difficulties were overcome, however, Kobe's foreigners were pleasantly surprised to find some attractions in the area. There was, for instance, the waterfall at Nunobiki, which they extolled extravagantly in guide books. It is still a tourist attraction. Old-timers used to recall how there was then no distressing smog, nor any shrieking klaxons to jar the ear. Instead, troops of monkeys gamboled blithely from limb to limb among the great trees around Nunobiki. Wild deer were abundant on Mt. Maya, while in nearby lowlands, mallards, snipe, and teal made merry, splashing the water or streaking through the rushes. Whole flocks of pheasants were flushed in the middle reaches of Minato-gawa, the port river, within a mile of what is today the neon-lit amusement center of Kobe.

To a generation brought up in the ways of modern Japan, it comes as a surprise to recall that feudalism was still in flower less than a hundred years ago. When foreigners first came to Kobe, there were no skyscrapers or automobiles, of course; criminals were still publicly decapitated in front of the prefectural office and on the beach at Wada Point. Samurai, carrying two swords, still wore quaint topknots, and the policy of national seclusion was still in force.

Only a few years earlier, in 1862, five young noblemen

risked capital punishment when they smuggled themselves out of the country through Nagasaki disguised as common sailors on a British ship. Then came swift changes for Japan. The Edo government collapsed in 1868, followed by Emperor Meiji's ascension to the throne. This heralded a new era of wholesale Westernization.

Shunsuke Ito, one of the five illegal emigrants, returned from England, where he had eagerly absorbed British culture to prepare himself for the task of rousing his country from its centuries-old slumber of seclusion. His earliest position under the new regime was that of governor of Hyogo. With the breadth of vision acquired by his contacts abroad, he poured his energies into a plan to develop Kobe into an international port. In this sense he was Kobe's greatest benefactor. He is more familiarly known today as Hirobumi Ito, Emperor Meiji's elder statesman and one of the great builders of modern Japan. Apart from having served several times as prime minister in the critical period after the Restoration, he is now most famous as the father of the Meiji Constitution, the charter which remained in force until 1946.

Among Kobe's more familiar landmarks are the Ikuta Shrine, Ichi-no-tani battlefield, Suma-dera temple, and Minatogawa Shrine. For centuries, the compound of Ikuta was an important rest station for travellers moving overland from old Hyogo to Osaka. Legend has it that Empress Jingu passed through the avenue in front of the shrine after having subjugated Korea in the third century. The place also marks the spot where an important battle was fought in the twelfth century.

In the fighting, the fifteen-year-old son of Kajiwara Kagetoki, plucking a spray of plum blossoms, thrust it into his quiver as he fired and charged on his horse into the enemy. Poetic-minded citizens of the locality are fond of recalling how the lad fought with both arrow and flower, and how the gods protected him from injury because his heart was as pure as the plum blossoms which he carried.

An entirely different aspect of the warrior's code of *bushido* was involved in an incident at Ikuta Shrine on February 4, 1868, the year Kobe was opened to foreigners. Lord Bizen, daimyo of Okayama, landed at Kobe that day from a junk on his way to Osaka to join the loyalist forces that had risen up against the Tokugawa regime which had ruled Japan for more than 250 years.

In the upsurge of antiforeignism then prevailing, these men were not only out to crush the shogunate that had permitted the hated foreigners to enter, but they vowed to throw out the white men altogether. Earlier the Bakufu had ordered all daimyo processions to bypass Kobe, a measure designed to avoid trouble in the vicinity of the foreign settlement, but Lord Bizen, a proud man, was in no mood to heed an edict of a regime he was out to overthrow. And so, in the fashion of the time, he and his party of 150 samurai swaggered along the prohibited route, his elite guards shouting stentoriously, "Down on your knees" to all and sundry encountered on their way.

The hotheads in the party clashed with some French marines guarding the settlement, and one of the Frenchmen was slightly wounded. Taki Zenzaburo, the officer in charge of the vanguard, lost his temper and gave orders to fire. This was the beginning of a skirmish in which his men and a contingent of American, British, and French troops exchanged shots around Ikuta Shrine. The firing was fast and furious. Bullets hit almost every object for hundreds of yards around, save only the combatants themselves. The old-fashioned soldiers of Bizen, being more adept at wielding swords than handling the new-fangled firearms, were easily routed. They hastily fled toward Kumochi and the Rokko Mountains.

As in most such comic opera battles, no one was hurt except an old woman who was accidently nicked in the leg. This Gilbert and Sullivan farce would have had a happy ending save for the fact that those were critical times for Japan, and the Bakufu was determined to stamp out the selfstyled patriots who tried to govern by assassination.

Since a number of foreigners had been killed only shortly before, there was genuine fear that this state of affairs, if left uncurbed, would lead to a wholesale massacre of foreigners. The emperor, from his palace in Kyoto, was prevailed upon to order summary punishment for all who committed atrocities.

Taki Zenzaburo, who had ordered the attack, was condemned to punishment of a particularly grim nature. As befitting the behavior of a samurai, he accepted all responsibility for the actions of his men. The Bakufu sternly ordered him to commit hara-kiri (disembowlment) in the presence of foreign representatives and high Japanese officials. His final act of expiation took place in the nearby Eifuku-ji temple. A. B. Mitford, who was with the British Legation at the time, gave this eye-witness account of the manner in which the impetuous samurai died according to the ancient code of his rank:

"Deliberately, with a steady hand, he took the dirk that lay before him; he looked at it wistfully, almost affectionately; for a moment he seemed to collect time, and then stabbing himself deeply below the waist on the left-hand side, he drew the dirk slowly across to the right side, and, turning it in the wound, gave a slight cut upwards. During this sickeningly painful operation he never moved a muscle of his face. When he drew out the dirk he leaned forward and stretched out his neck; an expression of pain for the first time crossed his face, but he uttered no sound. At that moment the *kaishaku*, who, still crouching by his side, had been keenly watching his every movement, sprang to his feet, poised his sword for a second in the air; there was a flash, a heavy ugly thud; with one blow the head had been severed from the body."

Eifuku-ji, the scene of this grim ceremony of death, was destroyed by B-29 bombers during World War II, but the grave of Taki Zenzaburo still remains in an obscure corner nearby.

Now we come to the landmark in Kobe which is perhaps more famous than any other. On the city's western edge rises Mt. Hachifuse, an elevation that crowds the narrow passage between its southern flank and the sea. The view from atop this peak is one of grandeur, with the entire city spread out below and the distant Awaji Island visible on any clear day in midchannel of the Naruto Strait. Near the base of Mt. Hachifuse close by the sea is Ichi-no-tani. Centuries of erosion have shorn the edges of this once-steep cliff, where a great battle took place one memorable day nearly eight hundred years ago.

The struggle for power was between the Taira and Mina-moto clans, which were engaged in a war that had gone on for many years. At first the Taira were in the ascendant, but by now the tide was turning, and the Taira were forced to retreat westward from Kyoto to Ichi-no-tani on the western edge of what is now Kobe. In their new capital they built a well-nigh impregnable citadel at a spot where high precipices guarded it from the north and west, the sea blocked attack from the south, and the only land approach in the east was heavily protected at its narrowest point by picked Taira guardsmen.

The Minamoto forces were under the command of two able generals, Yoshitsune and his brother Noriyori, who planned a simultaneous, two-pronged attack from the east and north. While Noriyori poised his troops for the lateral assault along the eastern pass by the sea, Yoshitsune, an unorthodox tactician, marched his men over the mountains to the north for a surprise attack from the enemy's

rear. There, on the night of Feburary 6, the hand-picked
cavalry force he commanded lost its way in the dark. To
extricate himself from his predicament, he sent out a
patrol, which brought back a local hunter for questioning.
To paraphrase an ancient document, the ensuing con-
versation went something like this:

> Hunter: Yonder is Hiyodori Pass, Lord. It is so sheer,
> that not a tree or a blade of grass grows on its side.
> Yoshitsune: Are there any deer around?
> Hunter: Yes, Lord. A great many of them. When
> winter comes, they arrive here from Tamba, and a few
> press on into Ichi-no-tani, but all return to Tamba
> in the spring.

Eyes glowing with satisfaction, Yoshitsune addressed
his troops in this fashion: "A deer has four legs, so has a
horse. If a deer can make the pass, so can we. Hunter, lead
us forward!"

When they reached the cliff's edge, dawn was just
breaking, and a vast array of palaces and pavilions lay
below, and over them a multitude of the Taira's red banners swam in the breeze. Beyond the city were the enemy's
encampments, where bonfires burned "like a sea of fire."
There, too, Yoshitsune descried the forces of his brother
Noriyori carrying flaming torches and poised to charge
the enemy. The day was February 7, 1184.

At Hiyodori Pass, Yoshitune gave the order to advance.
His men's horses, peering down, balked before the prec-
ipice. Quickly Yoshitsune placed two animals of his subordinates, a white mount and a bay, on the edge of the
cliff; then he gave the beasts a push. After thundering
down the steep slope, only the white horse—white was the
color of his Minamoto standard—sprang up from the cliff's
base to whinny at his master above.

A cry of jubiliation rose from Yoshitsune as he spurred

271

on his own mount and plunged down, landing safely at
the bottom. Others followed suit. In their eagerness to
outdo each other in negotiating the perilous descent, the
more ingenious young-bloods demonstrated some surprising tactics that have since become legend. There was
Sawara no Yoshitsura, for instance, who pulled the rump-
cover from his horse and, using it as a sled, slid down the
rocks like a man on a flying toboggan. But the glory of the
descent belongs to Hatakeyama Shigetada, the strongman
who demonstrated that day the purest flower of *bushido*
compassion. Dismounting, he is said to have addressed his
faithful horse in this fashion: "You have always served me
well in battle. Today I'll repay my debt to you." So
saying, the huge man is said to have strapped his steed
over his shoulders and carried the beast down the cliff,
using a *shii* limb for a staff.

Assaulted from the rear at a point from which they had
least expected an attack to come, the Taira forces were
taken by complete surprise. Pandemonium broke loose
within their ranks, and the beach sands that day ran red
with blood as the Taira men were cut down while trying
to flee on boats tied along the shore. Only a handful
escaped in that great battle of Ichi-no-tani, a turning point
of the fortunes of the once-powerful Taira clan.

Of the many other episodes of that battle, one deserves
special mention because it has become a perennial theme
of art and literature. The story concerns Kumagai Jiro
Naozane, Yoshitune's chief lieutenant. On the eve of the
battle, he bivouacked at the entrance to Ichi-no-tani. There
he heard someone playing a flute with great tenderness,
his whole soul wrapped in the music he was producing,
unaware of the morrow's battle.

When the battle was joined the next morning, Kumagai
placed himself strategically at the water's edge, waiting
to cut down the more famous of his enemies. Much to his
satisfaction, a Taira warrior at last appeared on horseback

in armor and helmet denoting a rank suitable for his attention. He was young and fleeing toward the sea.

Kumagai, a rough soldier, called out: "Young man, it is unseemly to turn away from an enemy. Come back and give battle like a true soldier!"

Taking out his fan, the Minamoto general then waved it as if to challenge the enemy to a duel. Although the fleeing soldier was deep in the water off-shore on his horse, he wheeled around and came charging. Kumagai was ready for him. After the first shock on horseback, the combatants rolled to the ground. Kumagai, a powerful swordsman who was a veteran of many battles, finally overpowered the other and was about to give him the customary *coup de grace*, when he suddenly realized that the enemy was a mere boy with the delicate features and proud bearing of an aristocrat.

"Tell me your name, and I shall save your life," Kumagai offered as he suddenly felt a wave of compassion at the sight of this lad who looked so much like his own son of about the same age.

The Taira soldier, however, stubbornly refused the older man's offer, saying, "You are my victor, and I am your enemy. Do your duty."

Kumagai hesitated an instant, torn between duty and compassion. At that moment a contingent of his own troops came galloping to the scene on horseback, and he knew it was now too late for him as their leader to save an enemy's life. It was only after he had slain the too-proud youth that he found that the enemy was none other than Mukan no Taibu Atsumori, the seventeen-year-old son of the Taira general Tsunemori. Among the slain enemy's possessions was a flute, and Kumagai now knew that it was Atsumori who had filled the air with music that previous night just before the battle.

Struck by the cruelty of war and deciding that the vanities of men are not the way of the Lord Buddha,

Kumagai shortly afterwards retreated to a monastery in atonement.

All this is told in the moving epic *Ichi-no-tani Gunki*, an ancient classic. One of the most famous dramas in the Noh repertoire derives from this story of Kumagai and Atsumori.

Near the old Ichi-no-tani battlefield today lies Suma-dera temple, where one may visit the pond where Atsumori's head is said to have been washed after it was severed. The compounds of the same temple also contain the mound under which the head was buried. It lies near the still-standing pine tree under which Yoshitsune, the commanding general, is said to have sat while the head was being examined for identification. The flute which Atsumori played on the eve of his death in battle is preserved here, as well as a portrait of him.

Nearer the center of Kobe is Minatogawa Shrine, where Kusunoki Masashige, a celebrated patriot, is enshrined. He is, in a way, Japan's counterpart of Nathan Hale of American history. As general of the loyalist forces defending Emperor Godaigo in the fourteenth century, Kusunoki is most famous for the statement that his greatest wish was to be reborn seven times to serve his emperor. He died with the inspired words on his lips, it is said, in the battle of Minatogawa, which took place where the shrine now stands.

Kobe is not only a seaport, a busy industrial center, but it also has claims to a rich historical past. Valor, gallantry, and compassion were not unknown to the men of Ichi-no-tani and their successors who fought, loved, and died here long before the port was established. Their deeds form a rich heritage for the people of this great city of Kobe.

16

Passing Pageant of
Nagasaki

FRUIT FROM THE GREAT GINGKO TREES IN
the yard of the ancient house fell to the ground each time
the wind blew. A frail old woman, with a face as sad as
the city's storied past, spoke dreamily of a time of vanished
glory.

"I planted those trees when I was a girl," she recalled.
"In those days these hills were dotted with fine houses,
and people were kinder. That was more than sixty years
ago. . . ."

This city of her birth, Nagasaki, is an ancient port,
industrially rich and noted in Japan for its cosmopolitan
outlook. It is city with a myriad historic memories, a city
whose hills once rang with the cries of Christian martyrs.
Old sailing ships of the seven seas came here bringing
spices, medicine, and learning, and took out gold from the
coffers of wealthy daimyo.

Against this background the white-haired woman

seemed like a fragment of that history. Although she spoke haltingly with a foreign accent, her quaint Nagasaki tongue was clearly intelligible. Her name was Felicita Smornova. Though she was approaching eighty-three, and bent with age, her mind was clear. He father was a Negro, she said, and he was a trader. Her mother was Japanese. Her husband was a Russian sea captain, now dead many years. She has a son somewhere in Brazil, a daughter in Holland. In her room in the great house built by her father nearly seventy years ago, she spends her lonely hours alone and aloof from the world.

Out in the yard, the expanse of the mellow sky was partially cut off by giant eucalyptus trees, cycads, banana trees, and the towering gingkos. Inside the building, paint was peeling off the walls, and the ceiling boards were warped with age.

"Old Nagasaki was nice," she recalled. "There are now only a handful of Russians in town. It's a lonely life for me, but I do not complain." Then, as if her words flowed from some harsh experience, she added, "War is bad."

Such houses as the one Felicita Smornova occupies still abound in the areas of the old foreign concessions, at east and south Yamanote. One of them is a delicately fashioned Western-style house on a height near the Cathedral of Uragami. With its slender pillars, tiled roof, and flower garden, this mansion has a certain air about it, as if it had once housed a minor nabob in the last days of the Edo shogunate. A board sign informs the visitors that the place has a "connection with Madam Butterfly." When questioned, officials at the local tourist bureau which put up the sign will not tell you just what that connection is, but the obvious implication from reading the sign is that Cho-cho-san once lived here.

Historically, there is no evidence to sustain the story that the tragic heroine of Puccini's famous opera ever lived here. In point of fact, this house, now vacant but preserved with care as a tourist attraction, was once the home of a Scotsman named Glover who came to Japan in 1859 and died a wealthy trader. He married a Japanese woman, and she bore him their only son, who committed suicide in World War II. There is no authentic fact of history that ties Glover senior with the heroine of the opera. The heart-warming scene in which the impetuous Pinkerton carries the willowy Cho-cho-san on their wedding day across the threshold of their new home took place elsewhere, if at all; certainly not in this house.

There are a number of versions regarding the origin of *Madam Butterfly*. An enterprising young journalist, Kiyoaki Murata, some years back delved into old records, both in Nagasaki and elsewhere. He came to the conclusion that truth favored the version which relates how a young U.S. Navy lieutenant once lived with a Nagasaki courtesan whom he had bought from a minor house.

Such an act, in the last days of the decadent shogunate, was common enough among the Japanese, but this could not be said of foreigners. At any rate, the story of this romantic fellow with a mistress got around quickly enough in the closely-knit, gossip-hungry foreign colony of the time. When the wife of an American headmaster who presided over the local Methodist mission school heard of it, she passed it on to the U.S. consul in Nagasaki. The latter in turn told the story, with embellishments, to his brother, John Luther Long, a novelist and playwright. Brother John, for his part, wrote a novel and called it *Madam Butterfly*. It appeared in the January, 1898, issue of *Century Magazine*. Subsequently David Belasco, the famous producer, staged a dramatized version of the tale in London. This production in turn inspired Puccini to write the opera of the same title.

Opera lovers from all corners of the world make pilgrimages each year to this famous landmark, and it seems a pity to have to disillusion them with the prosaic truth about this house. Mr. Murata, however, who visited the place himself, was entranced by its beauty and wrote: "Aside from the question of its history, the house on the hill commands such an enchanting view of the harbor where white ships sail on the cobalt sea on 'one fine day' that fact becomes unimportant to the visitor. The surroundings readily transport him to a real-life operatic stage, where he has the illusion of a willowy Cho-cho-san walking out of the dim interior of the building to the melody of the immortal aria."

Around Oranda-zaka (Dutch Hill) one can still find crumbling paving stones which were brought to Nagasaki from the nearby Amakusa and Goto islands more than a century ago. They recall to mind the era when the Dutch were the only foreigners licensed to trade with the Japanese. Now the ancient roads are badly in need of repair. The few stone slabs that still remain, though white when dry, take on a glistening blue cast when it rains.

The old Kojima road, once a busy highway between Nagasaki and Shigeki, used to echo with the clop-clop of horses and carriages during the early Meiji period in the nineteenth century. While carriages have long since vanished, the houses along the way still have straw sandals hanging over their backdoors, and flaming ivies greet the eye from every mud wall of storehouses along the way. Although most of the cobblestones have vanished, the sight of farm wives trudging homeward up the hill at sundown, with empty baskets on their backs after disposing their produce at the market, is practically identical with the scene a hundred years ago.

A legend says that hereabouts lies the spot where another famous girl of Nagasaki once lived, and left her name in literature.

In the summer of 1885, while the French warship *La Triomphante* was anchored in Nagasaki Bay, its tall commander lived in a small "paper house" on Dutch Hill with a local girl named Okane. The man was Luis Marie Julien Viaud. Later, after his return home, he published a novel based on his storybook sojourn in Nagasaki. *Madame Chrysantheme* was the title of the book, and its author is better known as Pierre Loti. Because of this, Oranda-zaka is sometimes referred to as Loti Hill. On many a summer day, so the story goes, the romantic Frenchman used to go down this slope on shopping trips, holding hands with his *petite Chrysantheme*.

More significant historically than any of these tender episodes was the advent in Nagasaki of Dr. Philipp Franz van Siebold (1796–1866), a distinguished scientist who acted as a "funnel" for Western knowledge entering the islands of Japan in the time of enforced Tokugawa isolation. Without exaggeration he may be termed Japan's father of Western science. He opened a clinic, taught classes, and battled with the obdurate shogunate in his efforts to open the door wider to Western knowledge. A young man of only twenty-seven when he arrived in 1823, he was a gifted scholar with diverse interests, which included biology, botany, zoology, history, and medicine. He was also a battler for freedom of the mind. A measure of his greatness is the fury with which the high authorities of the time persecuted him. They considered him a dangerous man and were convinced that the knowledge he disseminated— in fact, all knowledge from the West—would wreck the feudal structure they had so painstakingly built up, and thus undermine their source of power.

Under a pretext, they arrested him and finally expelled him, throwing thirty-eight of his pupils into jail. But the flame which he kindled was kept alive by his other pupils working underground. The very force of knowledge, which the shogunate had feared, eventually destroyed it, and Japan's doors were finally thrown open to the world after Perry's entry in 1853.

The story of Dr. Siebold is not complete without relating

279

his attachment with an eighteen-year-old courtesan named Otaki whom he met at a party given for foreigners. They lived together in a house on the mainland side of Nagasaki opposite Dejima, so the records read, and he was so devoted to her he named in her honor a hydrangea he had developed in his garden, calling it *Hydrangea Otakusa*. The flower is so listed in his book on Japanese flora.

After his expulsion in 1829, he returned to his native Bavaria, where he wrote many scientific books on Japan. Meanwhile, thirty years passed. Now sixty-three, he was unable to shake off the nostalgia that crept upon him. After the opening of Japan to the world, he set out to revisit his old haunts. As he arrived in Nagasaki in 1859, not only was Otaki waiting there for him in the tradition of a faithful Japanese wife, but his own son, now a grown man of over thirty, and his son's children all welcomed him.

We know just how this sentimental Bavarian looked at the time, with his bald head and white whiskers and dignified mien. There is extant an old daguerreotype of him, one of the first photographs ever taken in Japan. It shows him with his proud son, hat in hand, standing beside him.

As for Otaki-san, she too is a fit subject for an opera which some enterprising modern-day Puccini may yet write, preserving her lament, "Alas, those lost thirty years."

❀

The origin of the name Nagasaki dates from the twelfth century, when the Kamakura dictator Yoritomo gave the fief to a regional baron named Nagasaki Kotaro. For several centuries the place remained an insignificant village—and then strange bearded men arrived from the West. On August 15, 1549, the Jesuit father Francis Xavier landed in Kagoshima in southernmost Kyushu. Though he stayed in the country less than two years, he laid the basis for Christianity, which, at the height of the Christian zeal, had 300,000 converts.

Lord Bartholomew Omura, a daimyo enjoying lucrative trade with Portugal, was one of Nagasaki's earliest converts. In 1568 the first church in Nagasaki, All Saints Church, was set up in a converted temple. Meanwhile trade expanded with the West. The first Macao ship arrived in 1571, and in 1580 Lord Omura presented the port to the church domain. This "Little Rome" flourished, and Nagasaki became a receptacle for Western culture in Japan.

For centuries Nagasaki was the center of Occidental studies, because it was the only port of call for Western ships. Only the Dutch were allowed to trade here prior to Perry's arrival, and their stamp of culture on Nagasaki was impressive. Portuguese and Spaniards were expelled. Englishmen were here but briefly, pulling out of their own accord when the Bakufu clamped down on its policy of isolation. Much later dark-skinned Orientals from Southeast Asia arrived, and with the Meiji Restoration of 1868 came Americans, Frenchmen, Germans, and bearded Russians and turbaned Indians. General Ulysses S. Grant stepped on these shores with Mrs. Grant, and found in Nagasaki Chinese temples, Confucian shrines, Christian churches. Cultures throughout the world left an indelible imprint on the character of Nagasaki.

On a different plane, there is the unique Nagasaki style of cooking, which is a gourmet's delight. Even here is to be found the mingling of international flavor. *Castella* (pronounced "kasutera" by the Japanese) is a kind of sponge cake made from a recipe handed down by the Spaniards more than two and a half centuries ago; it is justly famous for its inimitable flavor, which is imparted by a secret mixing process. Nagasaki's most popular dish of exotic origin is *champon*, which is Chinese noodles modified to appeal to local taste, just as chop suey is an American hybrid of a Celestial concoction. It might even be said that Nagasaki itself is a bit like *champon*—a flavorsome city, with the tingling taste of Dutch beer on the side.

Aside from its historical and legendary interest, Nagasaki is important as an industrial center. It is a bustling commercial port, seat of the once great naval base of Sasebo, and since 1956 its shipyard has consistently been one of the most productive in the world. The mammoth battleship *Musashi* (which together with the *Yamato* was the largest ever built) was stationed here in the last stages of World War II, and the shed in which it hid from the far-ranging U.S. planes remained standing in the harbor for many years after the war as a monument to man's fanaticism and futility.

Then, of course, there is the statue. It is a gigantic figure in bronze, marking the dark hour when, at 11:02 a.m. on August 9, 1945, the second atomic bomb used in warfare exploded over the city, killing nearly eighty thousand people in one catastrophic flash. The statue towers forty-three feet in the air in an attitude of prayer, its right arm pointing upward in divine supplication. Although a serious symbol, the heroic figure seems to exert a personal fascination for many. An anonymous poetess quipped these lines:

> Though your eyes are sleepy
> And innocent of love,
> You are for certain
> A mighty handsome fellow.

Even more famous than the statue is Oura Church, built in 1865 commemorating the crucifixion of the early Christian martyrs. The story goes back to the time of Toyotomi Hideyoshi. For a while that sixteenth-century dictator was torn by his desire for profitable trade with foreigners and his fear of Christianity as a potential generator of strife within his Buddhist country. Ultimately he threw in his lot with his native religion, outlawing Christianity in1587.

Until 1596, however, Hideyoshi was half-hearted in carrying out his edict. Then in that year a Spanish sea captain was rescued off the coast of Shikoku and indiscreetly boasted that the Christian missionaries were being used to soften up Japan for eventual conquest by the Western powers. When Hideyoshi heard of the braggart's remarks, he exploded with anger. He ordered the summary arrest of twenty-four Christians, Japanese and foreign, in the cities of Osaka and Kyoto. He wanted to set an example for all who dared to ignore his anti-Christian edict. After their ears were cut off, the prisoners were led in chains on horseback through the streets of Osaka, Fushimi, and Sakai. It was midwinter, cold and windy, and the thinly clad believers presented such a pitiful spectacle that sympathizers who crowded the way offered them gifts of clothing which their guards, to their credit, did not have the heart to intercept. Two lay believers, while watching the procession, came forward asking to be included with the rest of the martyrs, making their number twenty-six in all.

Shipped off to Nagasaki, the group was taken to Nishizaka Hill, near where the station now stands. There they were nailed to a row of crosses, with crowds of Christians who had collected at their feet singing hymns and raising cries of lamentation. The martyrs suffered stoically, perishing with praises of the Lord ringing from their lips. In all the annals of Christianity the white flame of martyrdom never burned truer than here in Nagasaki on that fateful day, February 5, 1597. Among the martyrs were an archery teacher, an armorer, artisans, a doctor, simple townsmen, and Spanish missionaries. There were even two boys, aged twelve and thirteen. Later, when the news reached Rome, the whole Catholic world was grieved

by the martyrdom, and in 1627 Pope Urban VIII can-
nonized the twenty-six martyrs.

Oura Church, dedicated to the martyrs, commands a
view of Nishizaka Hill, and an impressive, uniquely modern
Christian chapel has recently been erected on the site of
the crucifixion itself. Another famous Christian landmark
of Nagasaki is the Cathedral of Uragami, which was almost
totally destroyed in the atomic holocaust of 1945. Rebuilt
in 1962, Uragami stands today as one of the finest Christian
cathedrals in the East.

For the early Japanese Christians, however, the main
historical drama was not the martyrdom of the twenty-six
Christians, but something that took place on the nearby
peninsula of Shimabara, south of the city of Nagasaki.
After Hideyoshi's death in 1598, Christian persecution
waxed and waned uncertainly for decades. Intrigues and
wars of succession absorbed all the attention of the rulers.
Then, in 1636, antiforeignism again became rife, and the
Edo government imposed a complete ban on all foreign
intercourse, with the death penalty for all who disobeyed.

As part of this policy the Shimabara fief was put in the
hands of a fanatical Christian-hating daimyo, Matsukura
Shigemasa, who replaced the Christian baron who had
ruled before. The new lord was a cruel, ambitious upstart
who vowed to exterminate Christianity within his domain.
Contemporary accounts record him as burning foreign
missionaries alive. He also had native Christians flung into
the fires of Mt. Unzen, a volcanic peak within his fief. His
son Katsuie, who succeeded him, went even further. In
addition to all other forms of torture, he extorted grinding
taxes from the Christian peasantry with such sadistic fury
that a ground swell of opposition mounted quickly into a
wave of desperation.

A man of incredible stupidity, who learned nothing and
cared less, Katsuie summarily arrested all who were unable
to pay taxes. He then wrapped them in rice-straw coats

284

called *mino* and set them afire. The contortions of these flaming victims came to be called the *mino* dance.

The year 1637 was a year of drought, with the hot sun drying up the land and people everywhere staring into the sky praying for rain. The prospect of crop failure, famine, and death looked down on them. In Shimabara the calamity was compounded by cruel taxes. For not having the wherewithal to pay the levies, the villagers were continually harassed by all sorts of means. In one instance the daughter of a farmer was "confiscated" like chattel, and tortured to death. To the hard-pressed peasants this was the last straw.

In the towns and villages the word soon got around in whispers of despair, and a few emboldened men held councils of war behind closed doors, urging action whatever the cost. A motley group of rude farmers, wearing straw sandals and wielding home-made weapons, made an ill-organized raid on the daimyo's stronghold, killing thirty persons, mostly lower-level officials. This was the spark that lit the conflagration.

At the news of the incident, mobs of men, women, old people, and children flocked to the scene, ready to join forces. Hundreds of them, thousands of them, singing hymns and chanting the name of Jesus and Mother Mary, marched to the castle town. Toward the end of October, 1637, they surrounded Katsuie's castle, burned the town and the local temple, and slew many officials.

Within the castle itself, the daimyo's men were divided in sympathy. Some wanted to fight, others recognized the validity of the peasants' grievances. The daimyo himself was away in Edo, the nation's capital, currying favor with the shogun.

Meanwhile, the sparks of rebellion spread quickly from Shimabara to neighboring towns, particularly on the nearby island of Amakusa. This whole area was Christian territory. The insurgents were fighting not merely against misgovernment, but also for their religion. They believed they would triumph because the Lord was at their side. They fought with incredible courage, giving up each life dearly but without regret, in the face of great odds.

Meanwhile, the daimyo of Amakusa, like his counterpart on Shimabara, was a rabid Christian hater. He is known to history as Terazawa of Karatsu. In his mission to exterminate Christianity he was at a disadvantage, for his fief was flooded with unemployed samurai warriors who had formerly been in the service of a daimyo who had been dispossessed because of his Christian faith. These roving warrior-adventurers now eagerly joined the peasants' cause in a gamble to win back their former status.

Amid the tumult of fighting, there arose a legendary figure to lead the rebels. His real name was Masuda Shiro Tokisada, but he goes down in history as Amakusa Shiro, from the name of the island from which he sprang. Self-educated and peasant-born, he was precocious as a child and fanatically dedicated to his faith. About him the historian finds much difficulty in weeding myth from truth, for the records abound with mysticism, legends, and ecstatic testimonies of the devout. One story says that he once opened the palm of his hand as he faced heavenward, and a dove lit on it, depositing an egg. Upon cracking this open, so the tale goes, he found a Biblical inscription inside. Another time, we are told, he walked on water from his native Amakusa to the neighboring Ito Island.

When the revolt broke out, Amakusa Shiro was only sixteen. In the fighting on Amakusa, the rebels killed the magistrate at Tomioka, and then crossed over the narrow strait to Shimabara. There they joined forces with the insurgents, who had already entrenched themselves behind the walls of the old abandoned Hara-no-jo Castle, a stronghold built years before by a famous Christian daimyo.

The fighting spread like wildfire. Soon the peasants had an army of 30,000, including 23,000 persons recruited from Shimabara and the rest from Amakusa and elsewhere. By now the shogun in Edo, the seat of the central government eight hundred miles away, had no illusions about the extent of the rebellion. To suppress it with the utmost dispatch and vigor, he hurriedly ordered to the scene a general by the impressive name of Itakura Naizensho Shigemasa, accompanied by a staff of aides. At the same time, he ordered the daimyo of all fiefs in Kyushu to raise punitive armies to converge on Shimabara.

The battles began in December. The defenders of Hara-no-jo Castle, in addition to being skillful campaigners, fought with great courage. Months elapsed, and there was no victory in sight for the government forces. Their casualties mounted. Edo became alarmed. To strengthen his forces, the shogun ordered to the scene Matsudaira Izu no Kami Nobutsuna, his right-hand man, as supreme commander.

When the field commander Shigemasa heard that he was about to be replaced, he vowed that he would reduce Hara-no-jo Castle before Nobutsuna arrived to take up command, no matter what the cost. He fought fiercely, even recklessly. The battle opened on New Year's Day of 1638 with a combined assault from many directions. More than four thousand of his men were killed, and he himself died in the fighting. So skillfully did the Christians fend off waves of attackers from behind barricades, that only a hundred or so of their own fighters perished.

Almost immediately after Shigemasa's death, Nobutsuna arrived. In the central government at Edo this man held the high office of Rochu, the foremost minister to the shogun. A cautious, wily man who took no chances, he was determined to reduce the castle by strategem, not by foolish expenditure of men. He had a plan. Not for nothing was he nicknamed "The Brains." He knew that the men who faced him were fanatical fighters, and he did not underestimate their capacity. He now proposed to starve the enemy into submission.

Nobutsuna asked a Dutch admiral with a warship at

the island of Hirado to bombard the Christian fortress. The Dutchman complied, since he was bent on reaping commercial profits by currying favor with the shogunate, even if this entailed fighting against his fellow Christians. The heavy gunnery was painfully effective. Starved, ill equipped, and in rags, the defenders were reduced to desperation. Nobutsuna, with an overwhelming force at his command, knew that the time to strike was at hand. Near the end of February he ordered a general simultaneous assault from all sides, and in the last furious fighting that ensued, Amakusa Shiro and his brave band were slain.

The debacle was complete. Some ten thousand men and women who fought under the Christian banner died that day. It was the last organized Christian resistance in Japan. To point out how well Nobutsuna's strategem worked, the well-equipped attacking forces suffered only 1,000 dead and 6,700 wounded, as against the virtual annihilation of the defenders.

For all their suffering and shedding of blood, Japanese Christians were practically wiped out that day—but not completely. Further isolated cases of persecution continued until the remaining believers went underground in the Nagasaki area and in the Goto Islands to the north. There they worshipped in secret, passing on their faith from generation to generation for more than two centuries.

Then in the Meiji era of the late nineteenth century the subterranean faithful emerged from hiding when freedom of worship was guaranteed after the Restoration. This preservation of a faith for so long under such adverse circumstances in Japan is one of history's remarkable events. It is also part of the Nagasaki story.

INDEX

Index

(Page numbers in italics indicate photographs)

290

◐ *The "weathermark" identifies this book as having been planned, designed & produced at John Weatherhill, Inc., 50 Ryu-do-cho, Azabu, Minato-ku, Tokyo. / Book design & typography by John W. Dower. / Halftone plates engraved by Misaki Seihan. / Composition & printing by Kenkyusha. / Binding by Okamoto Seihonjo.*

The main text is set in Monotype Baskerville 11 point with 1.625-point leading, the display lines in hand-set Bulmer italic 18 and 24 point, and the captions to the photographs in Monotype Baskerville 9 point with 1.3-point leading.

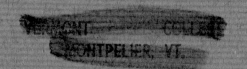
Date Due

AP 12 '93			
APR 22 '98			